Fire from Ashes

To Betty

From Ruth Bastede

Fire from Ashes

Ruth Isylma Bastedo

Faithful Life Publishers
N. Fort Myers, Florida

© 2010 Ruth Isylma Bastedo

ISBN-13: 978-0-9832039-1-9

Published by Faithful Life Publishers
3335 Galaxy Way, North Fort Myers FL 33903

www.FaithfulLifePublishers.com
editor@flpublishers.com

Printed in the United States of America
19 18 17 16 15 14 13 12 11 10   1 2 3 4 5

Table of Contents

Preface

Fire from Ashes is the story of my life and the subtle way my preacher husband wanted to kill my unborn child and then my mother.

I was born in St. Vincent & the Grenadines as the fourth of eleven children, a family of seven girls and four boys. I was a daughter of a well-known carpenter, and I attended the Georgetown Government School. At the age of seventeen, I married a Vincentian. A few months after our marriage we moved to Trinidad. Together, we had four children – two boys and two girls – but only know three of them. I'm so sorry that my husband's DNA runs through my children's veins. My prayer for them each day is for God to save them.

I pray that my children will be part of the chosen generation, the royal priesthood of God, and the blood of royalty will run through their veins, and that they will love their lives and be proud of their achievements. I dedicate this poem to my children.

It's Only For My Children
My tears can't flow I do not know
It's only for my children
My tears can't flow I do not know why
I saved them for my children
You can do to me what you want
I'll stand up, look at you, then bend down

Put on my shoe
Walk away, get angry
But my tears will not come through
It's only for my children
I was abused and still confused
I say, Lord, why can't I cry?
I must confess I had no success
As a person when you hear bad news you can cry, but not me
It's only for my children
My children were turned away from me
My pain is great, my heart aches
So then I can cry, I will not lie
It's only for my children
My father died, but I could not cry
I ask, Lord, why?
It's only for my children
If you want me to cry, just ask
How are your children? Are they coming your way today?
I'll feel my shattered spirit from deep inside
For broken heart is now shattered
My womb is feeling so empty
Four lives I wish I could shape
My children, I'll always love you all
Wherever you may be
My tears are for you, I want you to know.

After many years of abusive marriage, God made a way for me to escape. A woman, who was my son's teacher, took me to Canada, far away from my preacher husband. Yes, God is a way maker!

The Word of God says that if we are in Christ we are a new people, the old things pass away, and all things become new. This is true for me as well – old things are passing away and all things are becoming new.

I thank God for Mr. Joseph Lynch and his beautiful wife, Magdalen, who have made it possible for me to tell my story. Mr. Lynch is a very good friend and hard worker who will give his last to see a smile on someone's face.

Today, God has given me a wonderful husband, Michael Bastedo. God revealed him to me in my dreams two years before we met. He is helping me bit by bit to let go of my painful past. God is the God of second chances, and writing *Fire from Ashes* was healing to my soul.

I wrote this book to help open the eyes of those who are blind and those who are stuck in a similar situation. My prayer is that this book will open eyes to the demonic works of the devil. People have been destroyed because they lack knowledge.

And, to my children, whom I love with all my heart, this is to let you know why I was forced to leave.

Ruth Isylma Bastedo

1

Muzzled Souls

To God be the glory. If I can come through a life of abuse, anyone can. God is able.

I am writing today for all those preachers' wives who are afraid to speak out. I myself am a former preacher's wife who was secretly abused – physically, spiritually, and emotionally. I went through fifteen years of hell with my husband. I was not allowed to go anywhere without his approval, and if I did go out, a time limit was always given to me.

Many preachers use the pulpit to control those around them, and they use the Word of God to control their wives, who are the closest to them. If God wanted to make women footstools for their husbands, He would have taken a bone from Adam's toe to make woman. Have you read where God took the bone from? It was taken from Adam's side to create us. Who was the first person Jesus spoke to when He rose from the grave? Whom did he send to tell the brethren He was alive? Jesus knows He can count on women to speak out and joyfully spread the word. (John 20:16-19 & John 4:28-39)

My husband George was well known to all and had lots of followers. Many believed he was a good man and a man of God. Sometimes the women in the church would come to me and express their heartfelt wishes to have a husband like mine. If only they knew the hidden personality of their pastor! I thank God that He knew me before I was born. He called me for His own purpose; He has a better plan. My constant prayers for fifteen years were for God to make a way for me.

My preacher husband would have devotions every morning, sometimes for three hours, or for half of the day. The children and I would sit on a big couch, and he would either sit or stand in front of us. Our opinion was not valued, so we dared not utter a word on our own until he asked a question. One week his sermon topic was on Ephesians 6:12, a passage about wives submitting to their husbands, but to my husband it meant the woman was to give up her will. I was asked to give my will to my husband because he was the one God had called to reach the lost souls. Nowhere in the Bible does it say that women must hand over their wills. God did not take our wills from us when He made us, so why should any man own our wills? God said to submit, but He also said men should love their wives even as Christ loves the church and gave Himself for it. That type of love is sacrificial, not domineering and controlling.

Taking back my will almost cost me my life. I did not know George slept with a cutlass under his pillow because he had kicked me out of our bed years before when my feet touched his. From that point on, I was forced to sleep on the floor without sheets or pillows. One night, I took the cushions from the couch to make myself more comfortable. He ordered me not to touch his cushions as everything in the house belonged to him, even though I had received lots of the things personally as gifts.

———————◆◆◆◆◆———————

Whenever George wanted sex, he stood over me, pushed me with his foot, and said, "You! You! I am talking to you. Come up on the bed." Before I could reach the bed, he would pull my hands behind my back and then hold them as tightly as he could. Having my arms pinned behind me was very painful, but I didn't want our children to hear me cry out so I would breathe in as deeply as I could. As my husband forced himself onto me, he would call me a "stinking piece of meat" and tell me, "No man will want you. I just pitied you and married you." He said those things repeatedly and raped me as often as he wished. Yes, I was abused sexually – he utterly refused to treat me right or connect with me emotionally. As the years progressed, my lack of tears and unwillingness to struggle made him even more furious and forceful during our bedroom encounters. Over time, I learned to use the same psychological treatment he used on me. It was my weapon against him.

My husband often told me that since he was a man of God, I must call him "Lord." It would not have been hard to call him "Lord" if he was a loving husband and father to our children. So many times, I was beaten in front of my children and called all sorts of insulting names. George even gave the children a degrading name to call me. When he wanted to have some fun at lunch time, he would eat all the food I gave him, push the plate away, and then say, "This is not food but hog wash; I only ate it because I was hungry." After the laughter died down, he would eat some more.

My only comfort was prayer and my relationship with God. George would not allow me to have any friends; neither did he allow me to join the women's group at the church for many years. He continually said, "When you women get together, it troubles me," and "If you need to know anything, I will teach you at home."

Every Sunday morning before we left the house for church, George threatened us to the point that we were fearful to talk to anyone. He told me if anyone came up to me and asked any questions, I was to just smile, and so I did. Because of this, some thought I suffered from mental illness.

One Sunday, a group of ladies came to talk to me, and George appeared suddenly at my side. During our taxi ride home, he questioned me expecting a full report of all that was said. I told him the conversation, but he did not believe me. He thought I had told them about his attitude at home. His remark was "they only wanted to know your business." I told him to "stay away from those ladies." Within seconds, George punched me in the ribs, and tears immediately flooded my eyes from the excruciating pain. Getting out of the taxi was very painful especially since George made me carry the baby and the bag. The tremendous pain slowed me down as he walked along briskly with the other two children. Yet, I knew that one punch was not the end of the matter.

On our arrival home, he continued his abuse with his fist, hitting me all over the upper part of my body. When he finished, I pulled myself up and began cooking. My face was already turning black and blue. After pummeling me, George went to the bedroom to prepare for his Sunday night sermon. The children were playing which annoyed him, so he shouted. His shouts terrified the children so much they were quiet and the house became very silent. Only the noise of boiling water in the pot could be heard.

After a while the children began to whisper, which turned into giggles, and I heard footsteps coming out of the bedroom. What I feared was becoming a reality. George began to choke one of the children. I ran towards our eldest son and tried to pull his father's hand away from his neck. George then turned on me with his eyes as red as blood. He shouted, "Oh! You want to defy me and my orders around here?" I did not care what he did to me since I was determined that he must not hurt my son.

That afternoon we all got a good whipping with my preacher husband's custom-made rod. George was too angry to eat his dinner, so he went to church without eating. I could not go with him because my eyes and face were black, blue, and swollen. I was glad for the freedom to pray and write letters to God because I did not have anyone to talk to. God became my intimate friend. As I drew closer and strengthened my relationship with the Lord, I heard more and more from Him. It is such a wonderful thing when you can talk to the Lord and receive an answer. My times with Him fed my soul, body, and spirit.

While my husband attended Bible school, I encouraged him to stay on when he wanted to quit. I had hopes that Bible school would change him, but instead he became worse. One day, I told him that when he finished school, I would also like to attend. Thinking I would change my mind, he said, "Sure."

The day came when my husband completed Bible school and it was my turn to attend. I took money out of my own savings and paid the tuition fees. When I got home, I told my husband what I had done.

"Do you want to humiliate me?" he raged. "You can't read or write so how can you possibly attend Bible school?" I guess he had a short spell of amnesia because I was the one that helped him with his assignments at home. He continued, "If you want peace in this house you will ensure that you are here all the time, especially at nights."

I did not reply.

The semester for Bible school began. Every day was a battle as I was not sure of making it to school the next day. Some of the courses my husband had problems with were my best courses. They were easy for me because I had corrected and organized most of his notes. When he realized my grades were higher than his, he was very upset. One day before I left for classes, he slapped me in my right eye. My eye swelled immediately. Realizing I was determined to go to classes, my husband told me to cover it up with makeup, which he had previously forbidden me to use.

When I arrived at classes, I washed off the makeup and went to the dean. (The dean of the school had taught my husband.) I gave him details concerning the latest incident at home. He spoke kindly to me; however, I was not in agreement with him when he told me I should not have attended Bible school if my husband didn't want me to. When my husband attended school, I never tried to stop him, and I knew the consequences if I dared to say to him, "You cannot go to Bible school if you want peace in this house."

The dean came to our home that night, and George locked himself in the bedroom. I knew I would spend another night in the living room instead of on the bedroom floor. I clearly imagined the enormity of the abuse in store for me the day after, but, frankly, I did not care.

Early the next morning, my husband attacked me repeatedly with his fist. His major concentration was on areas that were already terribly swollen. God alone knows how I got out of the house. I immediately ran with speed to the home of our senior pastor and his wife. Blood was streaming down my face, and my clothes looked tattered because of the fight. I felt both brave and scared.

When I reached the pastor's home, I proceeded to expose the fact that I had been continually abused for over fourteen years, and I pleaded for help and a way out of my situation which had become extremely unbearable. The pastor refused to believe me even though he saw the condition I was in. I then asked him to go to my home and talk to my husband.

I thought it was fair to inform the pastor what to expect when he got there because George had said, "Anyone who entered his house [as a mediator] would be chopped as finely as possible until he/she gains the appearance of minced meat."

The pastor looked at me and said, "Oh yes!" Then with fear in his voice, he said, "I will send someone to talk to him." I told him I was going to report the matter to the police and let the law deal with my husband.

"Oh no!" replied our senior pastor. "You must not do that because the Bible says you must not take your brother to court."

I left the pastor's office and visited a sister who was going through the same sort of abuse but to a lesser extent than I.

"You are very brave to talk about your husband," she commended me.

"I am fighting this battle for all of us, and it is time for you to join me."

"I am not as brave as you, and I do not think that anyone would believe me. As a matter of fact, I tried telling someone in the church, and she went back and told my husband that I was trying to sabotage the work that he was doing for the Lord. From then on, I vowed to operate as though my mouth has a permanently closed zipper."

"Not only your mouth, but your whole body will be in a zipped bag."

She thought I was very harsh to her, but it was true. I felt that if we united against this evil that continually perpetrated against us, we would be brought safely through and become totally free from it.

On my way back from her home, I asked the Lord when He was going to take me out of my situation. The story of Lazarus came to me, reminding me of how God called us from death and gave us life, but many of us have bodies and souls in bondage. I knew God wanted mankind to live in liberty, but I couldn't because of the man I was living with, the same man everyone considered a pastor and thought of as a godly husband. Everything God made good in me, George discredited as though it was evil. All that I did under God's guidance was scorned by my husband. He forbade me from attending the ladies group at church, but I joined anyway. However, the entire group was in bondage, but I didn't hold back, and I let them know that we as women could go out and work. I not only said it, but I became the first to find a job.

When I started my job, it was hell at home, but I no longer cared. If George had been working for money and was a loving father to his children and wife, then I would have stayed home as he wanted me to. When the ladies of the group saw that I was working, they also decided that they too could find jobs and enjoy the freedom of earning money as I did.

One morning the children didn't have school, so as any loving mother would, I made breakfast and lunch while their father was comfortably lying in bed. Then I left for work. A little while after I arrived at work, my supervisor came over to me and said, "There is a mad man outside making a lot of noise, and he has two children with him. He has asked to see you."

Somehow I knew the man was George, so I decided not to go. However, my supervisor came over to me several more times. Finally, she said in my ear that I should go out to this man and talk things over because it was creating a scene at my place of employment. I turned off my sewing machine and stepped outside. As I exited the building, I turned around to see my supervisor standing at the door watching to see what would happen.

George stood there pointing to the children and shouting, "These children are your responsibility!" and then he walked away. I had no choice but to ask my supervisor's permission to leave in order to attend to the children and let her know that I would report for work the next day.

At home I played some games with the children while their father rested on the bed. When he realized I was ignoring him, he came out and said, "Let me tell you something…"

7

As soon as the words came out of his lips, he grabbed me by my hair and dragged me inside the bedroom. I immediately placed myself in a fetal position in order to protect my face because I knew from experience that my face would be his prime target. He started beating me while saying, "You want to make me look small by going to work. Do you want to wear the pants? There is only one man in this house and I am that man."

I was beaten all over my body except my face. I used all of my ability to concentrate on staying in that fetal position so as to preserve my face. I felt it was necessary to do that and although it was a small victory, I felt a bit triumphant. I numbed myself and stuck to my inner resolve to cease from crying when he physically abused me.

The next day I prepared the children for school, dropped them off, and went to work. When I walked through the doorway at work, I could sense everyone looking at me. I thought to myself that it was a good thing that they could not see the evidence of abuse on my body. I thanked God that my face was not bruised.

Later on during the lunch hour, I spoke with Peggy, a childhood friend of mine who was also working at the factory. I asked her if I could stay at her home and she agreed. I spent the following week at Peggy's house.

On Friday after I was paid, I went to see my children and discovered that they had not eaten or had a bath for the entire week. When I entered the house, my husband shouted, "I don't want you here!"

I proceeded to grab my big brown suitcase into which I hurriedly threw some clothing. I kissed my children goodbye, balanced my suitcase on my head, and walked down the hill feeling both embarrassed and relieved. I could have taken a small bag and stuffed it with my meager belongings, but I wanted to be seen so as to make a statement to the other ladies in my neighborhood that we could still obtain victory after much hardship and pressure. One of them came up to me and congratulated me on my bravery. As I passed the standpipe, the crowd standing there stared at me in amazement. I saw that some were laughing uncontrollably, but I pretended not to notice. That afternoon marked the beginning of my freedom from abuse. Arriving at the end of the street, I took a taxi to

Peggy's house. I thanked God for providing me with a safe place for me to stay.

I spent another week at my friend Niasa's home. It was the longest and most unbearable week I ever spent because I feared that my children would be left to starve to death. I prayed before I returned to my home and all the way to the house. As I walked up the hill, my family saw me; they began shouting and jumping.

My husband came towards me with outstretched arms saying, "Welcome back." I was in awe. Was it really me he was talking to? With his arms now around me, he took me inside and said, "I didn't mean all the things I have said to you, I really didn't want you to leave." He made no mention of the beating so I guess he was never sorry for what he did to me. In my mind I wondered if he was planning to do me harm. I told him that if I were to stay, I would be working. He agreed with a tight clench to his teeth.

So, I stayed and on Monday went to work. Upon entering Niasa's home to retrieve my belongings, she began laughing and commented, "I know you can't do without him." After work I took my suitcase back home.

I was able to work from then on without a problem, and we were able to eat each day and save a little in the bank. My paycheck proved to be beneficial to me and my family. Things were okay for a while; then as suddenly as an eruption from a dormant volcano it began all over again. The beatings and verbal abuse doubled.

————◆◆◆◆◆————

I can remember the day my mother looked at me and asked why I allowed myself to be bullied and abused for so long. She was aware of my childhood when I would usually find a way out of those types of situations. I told my mom, "First, I'm not that person anymore because I let God do my battles, and secondly, this is not any ordinary person I'm dealing with. This man behaves as though he is strengthened by demons. This fight is not with flesh and blood."

George was the type of person who would give me a black eye, then turn around with a subtle smile on his face and ask who did that to me. One year, he gave me two pair of panties for my birthday. (I appreciated his gift because my only other underwear was the top of pantyhose with the legs cut off.) After returning from church one Sunday, I was changing while he sat on the bed. He looked at me and asked, "Are you finished changing?"

"Yes."

"But you haven't taken off the panty I bought for you. It is not to wear at home but only when you are going out of the house."

"Did you buy it for me," I questioned as I looked him square in the eyes, "Or for you?"

The next thing I felt was a lash to my face and his hands pulling my panties off my body.

————◆•)◆(•◆————

When I asked my husband, who was also a tailor, to sew me nice clothing like what he made for other women in the church, his reply was "You are like a piece of stick and have no shape so these type of clothes won't look good on you."

I decided to sew my own clothes, but George did not like anything I made. Sometimes I would make beautiful clothes, such as knee length skirts and short-sleeved tops. He never permitted me to wear them and repeatedly told me that he thought I wanted to dress like Jezebel's daughter. As long as a woman is dressed modestly and looks good, I never saw the need for wearing long dresses to cover our necks and heels. Our husbands and boyfriends just go to church or the workplace and look at other women who are dressed modestly, but not covered from head to toe.

Red is my favorite color, but I was not allowed to wear red because George claimed it was the devil's color. He also said that any time I wore red something bad would happen to me. I knew I looked very nice in my red outfits, and he knew it too. People often complimented me whenever I wore red, and he hated hearing the compliments.

One day we were going out, so I put on my red top. George began to argue and said, "I told you not to wear that devil's color! You are not coming behind me in that red top."

This time, I decided to not change my red top as I normally would have, so off we went by taxi. I was sitting next to the window, and the midday sun was piping hot. I decided to open the window. As I tried to slide open the glass window, it shattered.

"Do you see what you did? Destroying people's property!" shouted George. "I told you, anytime you wear red, something bad will happen to you."

The driver stopped the taxi, came to my side, and said, "Don't worry; this window was sticking for a long time. I knew this would happen."

As we continued on our outing, I asked myself a question – Why didn't my husband think instead of the significance of red to a believer? Anytime I think of red, I remember the blood of Jesus that was poured out on Calvary's cross for my sin.

Sometimes my husband would ask me to hand him a blue button while he pointed to a white one. I would tell him that the one he was pointing to was white, and he would insist that it was blue. In order to refrain from a senseless argument, I had to agree that the button was blue. I knew that basic childhood learning included color differentiation, and I was way beyond the basic.

———◆◆◆◆———

You may be wondering if my husband was abusive before we were married and the answer is: Yes! You may also wonder why I couldn't see him for who he truly was. I was fifteen years of age, had never dated, and was never told what to look for to determine if a man was good or bad. Plus I desperately wanted to say goodbye to my abusive childhood home.

During our pre-marital times, I certainly wished that I had some counseling from a fellow believer. Because George and I met in church, I never asked the question, "Does he go to church?" Unfortunately, he sounded and talked like a sheep, but he never lived like one. In the house he was very uncomfortable in the sheep's skin and felt more at home in the wolf's clothing. The sheep's skin was his outer garment for the streets and church. I was too young and naïve before we were married to fully understand the difference.

My advice to young ladies who are head over heels in love with handsome guy is to take time to get to know the person you are about to share the rest of your life with. Find out:

- What is his background?
- What is the history of his father? Is he an alcoholic, a woman's abuser, or user?
- What is the level of his education and the extent of his knowledge of life?
- Do a thorough investigation of him.
- Educate yourself about certain signs and signals that might be warning signs.
- Observe his social life.
- Find out about his friends and their interactions
- Observe his family life and their level of respect for one another.
- Never try to change a man because he has to change for himself. Who you marry is who you will have for the rest of your married life.
- Don't be afraid to ask questions and be sure to mentally note the answers.
- Check his emotions and be aware of subtle or overt anger.
- Does he want everything to be his way all the time?
- Does he talk his way out of situations instead of taking responsibility?
- You may feel like the devil's daughter-in-law if you marry someone who behaves as his son. Find a Christian with integrity and sound moral values who can be a trusted friend, confidant, and prayer partner.
- Seek the Lord over and over until you are sure that this is the one that He has prepared for you.

It does not matter how long it takes you to find a good man. Wait on the Lord's timing; you will find the one whom God has prepared until death sets you apart instead of one who wants to bring death upon you.

For women who grew up with physical or emotional abuse during their childhood and teenage years, fleeing the home situation to enter into a marriage may seem like a relief. However, for those who marry an abusive husband, their troubles will only be beginning. Once a woman is married, she is on her own. I can remember my mother giving her speech at my wedding. She said, "When you have problems, don't run back home to me. Stay and bear them." I felt that day like I was cut off from my family, and I was on my own, since my mom was the only one who listened to me. Who else could I turn to?

Ladies, don't try to keep what you do not have. Learn to cut your losses. God will make a way. The door of liberty is open for men and women.

―――――◆•◦•◆―――――

My preacher husband blamed everyone and took absolutely no responsibility for the breakup of our marriage. He could never imagine that I was indeed a person of strength or, at least, well able to make decisions. Men who are possessive never seem to think that their wives are capable of thinking.

Through the years of abuse, Jesus became my only friend; I see Him as a friend that cares and comforts me. God is able. I'm not saying surviving and fleeing from the abuse was easy, but just remember you and I serve the same God of Abraham, Isaac, Jacob and Joseph. I serve the Lord Jesus Christ, and I know He can and will make a way out for anyone who is trapped.

God says He will give us the desires of our heart when we believe, but only according to His will. The only way our prayer cannot be heard is by sin. Live clean before God in spite of your abuser's lies and insecurity. Remember the devil is the accuser of the saints of God. Many women take their own lives – that is not the way to escape. Wait on God, and He will make the way out. Remember that even the longest night will always give way to daylight.

Even though I am now free from the abuse, I can still recall all that my preacher husband did to me.

2
The Beginning

God saved me at the early age of nine years old, but no one knew until I was fifteen when I openly said so at the church. I kept silent because of the many dark things that surrounded my life from an early age.

I always told my best friends that I would not be wayward on the streets or be like some of the other girls in the village. I told them that the only way I was going to leave my parents' home was by marriage. I had three offers. My mom chose George, a preacher, for me. She said he would be just fine for me, and she even warned me not to give him any trouble.

What my mother called "trouble" was my tendency to be very outspoken and not allow myself to be bullied. It did not matter how big and tall you were – I still wanted to fight. My mom though that I should be silent even when my sister overstepped the boundaries and behaved unmannerly towards me at the dinner table. All of my siblings were caught up in the manipulation. I even remember being stoned by them and being told that I should not retaliate because I was a Christian. Why should ten siblings be allowed to bully one sister?

When George and I first met, I was about fifteen years old, and he was over ten years older than me. One Saturday afternoon, he visited my mother. He told me to let her know that he was coming to talk with her. That day my mother cooked and asked him to stay for dinner. Before dinner, they sat down and laughed, talking like old friends. While I was passing through the living room, I heard him ask my mom how many Christians were living in the home.

"One and a half!" my mom shouted out. Then she pointed at me and said, "She is the one, and I am the half." George then asked the question over, and my mom began laughing and said, "The young lady you want to marry is the half."

When I heard her words, I felt like a rug was pulled out from under my feet. He later told me that my mom wanted him to marry my younger sister because she thought he was too good for me.

When it was time to eat dinner and everyone was at the table, George excused himself and went outside. He stopped under the banana tree next to the house, trying to hide himself. He did not know that I was looking through a hole in the door. The tree was close to the house, and I wondered why he would go there to urinate when he could have gone to the back of the house. I continued watching him when he did the strangest thing. He began digging out his ear wax and eating it, doing one ear and then the other! His fingernails were very long so he did not have any trouble getting the wax out. I've never seen anything like it in all my life, and to me, it seemed as if he had not cleaned out his ears for a long time. After eating his ear wax, he came in, sat at the table, and, with a big smile, said "Something is smelling good."

I sat next to him and watched as he began to switch the plates and drinks that were set in front of us. (My mom did not see George do this.) I sat back and enjoyed my big plate of food originally meant for George. After dinner he stayed for a long time talking with my mom. My mind raced with all I saw in that short space of time. I could not tell my mom about the ear wax because she too was captivated by his charisma and saw him as specifically handmade by God Himself. I also knew that if I told any one of my six sisters that she would in turn tell my mom who would tell George, so I kept quiet.

One day ten years later, when George was telling me how clever he was, I finally understood why he ate his ear wax before eating my mother's food.

"No woman could trap me. I am too smart for them," he said. "Whenever I had a relationship with a girl and had to eat from her or the mother, I did not clean my ears for weeks beforehand. My ear wax is my antidote to protect me from any harm."

Needless to say, I gained the awareness that superstition keeps company with stupidity!

He also said that he knew what he was looking for in a woman and stated that he never wanted a lady who was knowledgeable of the facts of life. He wanted someone that he could mold and shape to be what a good wife should be. He wanted to be the teacher, and he sure did get what he was looking for and more with me. I was handed to him on a platter.

One Saturday, he came up to the country and asked my mom if he could take me for a walk and she gave the okay. On our way back darkness was falling and we were coming close to a deep corner with a big tree at the side of the road. George stopped under the tree and called me close to him. He placed my back up against the tree, and then pressed his body against mine. His large lips were over mine, but I stood there not knowing what to do – I had never been kissed before. He began pulling on my lips when all of a sudden I felt like live wires in my body were sparking. He kissing me even harder on my lips, and I felt something running from my feet to my hands, head, neck and arms. I jumped away.

"What were you trying to do to my body?" I asked him.

"What are you talking about?" he laughed.

The remainder of the walk back home was not pleasant to me anymore. George tried talking, but my answers were short. He took me back home and said goodnight.

The next day I went to see his cousin to ask her why George was trying to take over my body. I told her what he was doing and how my body reacted. She threw herself down on the bed and laughed. I sat there until she was through. She wiped the tears from her eyes as she tried to talk.

"He was kissing you and your body was responding. Next time try closing your eyes and opening your mouth."

The next Saturday George came up to see me again, and after talking to my mom, he told her he was taking me for a walk. We walked the same path again, and I thought to myself, "I will not look like a fool again. I know what to do now."

We stopped next to a large stone this time, and as George pulled me close to him, I opened my mouth wide and tightly shut my eyes. I stood there in silence for a few moments, and then opened my eyes to see him looking at me. As he pulled me close again, I again opened my mouth and closed my eyes.

"Why is it that every time I try kissing you, you start yawning?" George demanded.

I answered with the only thing that popped into my head. "I'm hungry."

We walked briskly home.

I could not wait until the next day to give his cousin a piece of my mind! After completing my chores at home, I went over to see her. We went to her bedroom and closed the door.

"You made me look like a fool again!" I told her as I described what happened step by step. She laughed as I tried to explain what George was doing to me. I thought I knew all about the birds and the bees, but I did not know a thing.

I was still living in the country with my mom, who never told me anything about the facts of life. George was the first guy I walked the street with without having my mother threaten to break my arms. I always told my cousin that the man I would have sex with must be my husband because I knew that God did not approve of sex before marriage. She said I was missing out on real fun and even gave me a deadline when I should be having fun, as she put it.

I got a job in a garment factory in town ten minutes away from my boyfriend's house. I thought it was God's way of telling me that George was the right one. I didn't have a place to stay, so he arranged for me to stay with the pastor and his wife, who didn't have any children as of yet.

During the first weekend that I stayed at the pastor's home before beginning my new job on Monday, George took me to meet his father, and then his sisters. None of his sisters were pleasant or welcoming. I did not know at the time that he had told them he was about to get married, so they all must move out of his house as soon as possible.

On Sunday night he preached at church, and since no one in the church had cars, we all walked home in groups. It was an hour's walk to the pastor's home, but we walked slowly and it took two hours for us to get there. The distance seemed short as George chatted incessantly about himself and his various abilities. I did not have a chance to talk, and he was glad that I was listening.

During that first week when I was trying to figure out what was going on with our communication, I developed a way to shut him out without listening or saying anything. I just kept a wide smile on my face. He loved to hear his own voice. Whenever he was preaching, he would make sure he had everyone's attention. If a baby was crying, he would look at the mother with a scolding look on his face as a sign of displeasure, and she would remove the child.

He also viewed the pulpit as a place to model his self-made suits as a way of advertising and attracting more tailoring business. He was one of the few tailors that always dressed neatly. He always said that if anyone stood out in the crowd, that person would be him. He was a perfectionist when it came to how he dressed.

One day I went and bought a piece of fabric to make an outfit for myself. I bought enough so that he could make a shirt as well. When I told him he could have a shirt too, he laughed at me, and said, "I must always be one of a kind. I can't wear the same fabric you are wearing. People will not be able to see the uniqueness in me."

Instead, he took the fabric and made a long-sleeved top and skirt reaching my ankle. That was the first thing he ever made for me. When I wore the outfit to church, he told me I was dressed like a perfect lady should. I looked like a grandma trapped in a teenager's body. All I had going for me was my long hair which I styled well. When George realized I was getting a lot of compliments on my hair, he told me to stop straightening my hair because God did not love that.

One afternoon he called me over to his home and opened the Bible. He showed me the passage concerning Jezebel saying that she dressed herself so as to attract men. He went on to say that I should just wash my hair and pull back it back into a ponytail. Can you imagine an African woman with long hair just washing her hair and having it in a ponytail all the time?

My whole outlook had changed by this point; I had the face of a thirty-year-old woman to match the clothes that he made me. George said I was looking modest. However, I no longer received compliments. I felt like a shadow. I was there but not being seen clearly for who I was. I began to cry and pray in the night when I was alone. I asked God, "If you say, Lord, I must let my light shine, how can I do it when I am not being seen or heard? Why must a woman be less than a man? How can I do what you want me to do when I have no rights?"

I began to tell George all that the Lord was telling me and what he wanted to tell others in the church. George would preach about what I told him, and then he would say to the congregation that the Lord had spoken to him. The Lord showed me things about people in the church, and I would then tell George; I was always on target. He would then approach the congregation, say that the Lord had spoken to him to let them know, and would tell them what the Lord had shown him about that person. He never let them know I was the one to whom the Lord had spoken to carry out His message.

The Lord gave me another insight into people too. When I shake a person's hand, I know things about that person. When I told George about it, he said that I should not tell anyone. He introduced me to all kinds of people and then asked me what feedback I got. Then he met with that person behind my back saying God had shown him things. He saw time and again that what I said came to pass.

19

George never let me hold his own hand, but I did not have to hold his hand to know that something was wrong. I could not do anything about our relationship; my mother believed in him and had already told me not to be rude to him. She felt that it was rude to let it show that I disagreed.

I started making more money at my job once I realized that I could work through my lunch hour, but I could not save any of what I made. One Saturday morning, bright and early, I heard a small voice calling outside, "Good morning, good morning." The pastor went outside to see who it was, and then there was a knocking on my bedroom door. When I answered, he told me that someone was outside for me. I went to the front door and there was a tiny girl about the age of seven. I knew that I had seen her face somewhere but could not place who this child was. I asked what her name was and what she wanted. The little girl placed her hands over her mouth, rested her head upon my chest, and began to mumble something. I bent over and asked her to remove her hands from her mouth.

"It is okay, you can talk to me," I said.

She looked at me and quietly said, "Grandpa said to send some more money for him."

Then I remembered the tiny voice that was calling "Grandpa, Grandpa," when I went to see George's father. I went to my bedroom and returned with twenty dollars and placed it into her hand. I told her not to stop and play, but to go straight home to her grandpa. I soon discovered that giving money to my boyfriend's father was one of the worst mistakes I ever made.

The next Saturday it was the same thing over again, but this time he said the amount he wanted. This went on for a month until I told his son. He felt so ashamed and told me not to send any more money to his father because he looked after his father. The next time the father sent for money, I sent a message that I did not have any. He sent a message back asking for me to come and see him by myself.

I waited until the sun was almost down. I did not want to climb the big hill up to his house in the hot sun. So, in the cool of the evening, I went up to see my boyfriend's father. He was sitting outside on a wall. I walked up to him, smiled, and greeted him. He did not answer me, so I sat next to him on the wall and asked, "How are you?"

"Let me tell you this," he said as he turned to me, "My son gives me money every month, and if you want him to marry you, then you have to look after me too. And don't think if he marries you, he will stop looking after me." He went on to say, "I can remember going to the river to wash his dirty diapers. He was the only one who I wash for."

I sat there looking at him until he was silent. I knew that he was just like his son when he was talking, expecting me to stay silent, not interrupt, and wait to ask questions until when he was through. As he stopped speaking to get some air, I told him that I did not intend to support him. I told him that his son was a grown man and knew what he wanted.

Surprisingly, George's father was relieved to hear those words. He then sent the little girl inside for some mangoes for me. He did not send them with the child before because there was no money. I accepted the bag of mangoes and said it was time for me to leave. He thought I was about to give him money, but I did not.

When I reached the big hill, I stopped and turned the bag of mangoes upside down. I watched the ripe mangoes roll down the hill. They were a gift that came with a price, and I didn't want the gift. I knew that if I told him I did not want his mangoes he would have been even angrier with me. I was glad no one was around when I let the mangoes roll down the hill because everyone in the village knew him.

On the top of the hill was a large mango tree. When I reached the bottom of the hill, a lady was picking up my mangoes. I smiled and said, "Good afternoon."

"I am the first person to eat from that tree on the hill," she said to me.

"Good for you!" I told her as I laughed.

She did not know that the mango tree grew a different kind of mango, and I was the one to roll the mangoes down the hill.

21

On my way home, I passed George's house. I stopped and let him know what his father was up to. Again, I saw the shame on his face. The only thing he said to me was that his father was an old man who loved his son. He told me not to let him push me around and stop giving him money. He told me that he would talk to his father again.

If I had more experience in the world, I would have seen what to look for in George's background. His father and mother had twenty children, yet none of them stayed at home with him because of his attitude and his controlling spirit.

3
Sowing Sour Seeds

Early one Saturday morning, the sun shone through the window pane and I turned my face to escape the full sunlight. I knew it was still early since the lady of the house, who was an early riser, had not left her bedroom yet. I told myself that it was my day off, and I must make the most of it. I was not going to go anywhere, and planned on cleaning my room and returning to my bed. So I did so, until twelve o'clock, when George came home from work and sent someone to let me know that we were going out. I got ready and went up to his house.

I knocked at the front door, but there was no answer. The front door was open, so I pushed my head in and called out, "Is anybody home?"

"Come in and have a seat," a voice answered from the bathroom. Two minutes later, he came out with a big smile on his face and a towel around his waist.

"Where are your sisters?"

"We're all alone," he replied with a grin on his face. "I am about to take a shower, but I have to tell you first how nice you are looking."

When he started making advances towards me, I tried running out of the house, but he caught me in front of the house door. He grabbed my skirt, pulled me to him, and placed his large lips over my mouth. I began to push him away. He pulled my hands behind my back, I fell to my knees in pain, and he forced me to the ground. Of course, I did not know what date rape was at the time, but I was experiencing it.

With one of his hands at my neck and the other tearing off my clothes, he sat on my legs. His eyes were as red as blood, and thick drops of sweat ran from his skin like raindrops on a windowsill. He choked me during the entire episode as my head hung out of the front door. I could not speak and fought for air to breathe.

After he was through raping me, he said, "Don't worry, next time it will be better."

I sat there still trying to get myself together.

When he saw that I was upset, he said, "This is all your fault anyway. What do you expect when your hair is in that style and you dress so nice? It just turned me on. If you tell anyone," he continued, "no one will believe you. You're just a country girl and I'm a preacher. Not even your mother will believe you because she loves me."

I felt so small and ashamed. George then pulled me to my feet and looked me in the eyes.

"Do you know that I just pitied you? That is why I let you be my girlfriend! You are to be glad I have chosen you."

Looking at his bloodshot eyes, I could not speak a word. I did not know what to make of the situation.

We both heard footsteps walking at the side of the house, coming towards the front door, and George let me go from his grip. He dashed to a chair at the table and sat with his hands covering his head. The footsteps came to the front door, and then his brother entered the house. I was still rooted to the same spot when his brother greeted us, "Good afternoon."

No one answered. He then asked what was going on. At that point George raised his head from the table, and looking at his younger brother, innocently asked, "What are you talking about?"

"Why are your eyes so red?"

His brother's question was the last I heard as I dashed out of the house and ran down the street holding my torn skirt. As I entered the pastor's home, his wife was sitting in the living room. She turned to me and asked, "Why are you back so soon?"

I did not give her an answer but went straight to my room, locked the door, and sat in the corner. I sat there in silence, hearing my preacher boyfriend's voice in my head, repeating all of the things that he had said to me. "It's all your fault… I pitied you. That is why I let you be my girlfriend…No one would believe the country girl…country girl… country girl." I sat in the corner for a long time.

When the numbness started leaving my body, I started feeling pain between my legs and arms. I remembered his cousin saying that sex was fun, but it was not fun for me. I did not realize George took something from me again that could not be replaced.

I decided to take a shower and then went into the living room. Thankfully, no one was there. The pastor's wife was in the kitchen, and as she passed by from one side of the kitchen to the other, she saw me sitting there. With a big smile on her face, she asked, "Why are you back so soon? Was there a fight between you two love birds?"

I knew that they did not want me for their star preacher; they even told him not to get involved with a country girl. I told her to sit next to me, which she was happy to do because she knew she was about to hear something juicy.

"How well do you know George?" I asked her.

"For years. What did he say to you? Did he say it was over between the two of you?"

"No."

Her bubble burst, and her smile changed. She could see that I was in pain, but all she wanted was to hear something juicy so that she could tell everyone they were right. I was not about to let them rejoice over my pain, so I kept quiet.

"Did you see him with Ann?"

"Who is she?"

"Ann in church."

"You mean," I asked as I turned to her, "The girl without front teeth that always wants to sing?"

"Yes, that's the girl he is in love with."

I did not say another word to her. Just then, her husband walked through the front door, and she called him into the bedroom. I sensed that they were having a discussion about me. Shortly afterwards, he stormed out the door. I believed I knew where he was going. He came back very late.

The next day was Sunday, and we all got dressed and walked to church in the morning. The pastor and his wife did not say anything to me. I suspected that the pastor's sermon about "who is your friend" was targeted at me. George was sitting at the front, nodding his head in agreement with every word out of the pastor's mouth. At one point, the pastor asked the question, "Guys, how do you know your girlfriend? Delilah killed a great man of God and he was killed because he did not listen to his elders." I had heard enough of the pastor's sour seeds that he was planting and decided it was time for me to ignore the sermon. I took my hymnal, began to look for all the zeroes, and then fill them in page after page. I did not hear when the pastor asked everyone to stand and turn to a song in the hymnal. All of a sudden I heard the congregation singing the last song before the altar call.

"There are some of you in here that need to repent of your sins, the sin of lies. There are those of you who want to destroy other people's lives. You know who you are; the Lord knows who you are too." The pastor continued "Come, come with heads bowed and eyes closed. There is someone here that needs to be in front here, and this is your last chance to make things right with God."

I noticed that the pastor's voice was getting closer. A small voice in me told me to open my eyes and see where he was, and so I did. The pastor was standing in the middle of the church next to my bench. No one went to the altar, so he began praying for people who were close to him. I knew he would eventually come to me, so I walked out on the other side. I stayed outside until everything was over.

After the service was over, small groups of people stood around talking. I felt so guilty and ashamed, thinking that everyone was talking about me. I retreated from the churchyard and proceeded walking home all alone. I heard a van coming towards me, so I stood at the roadside to make room. Looking at the van, I saw the pastor, his wife, and my preaching boyfriend inside. They did not stop for me although they knew that we were all going to the same place. But why would they stop for me when they were trying to keep the good guy from the bad country girl?

The sun was very hot, so I stopped to rest under a big mango tree that was close to the road. I wondered what to do, knowing that the pastor and his wife did not like me and would ask me to leave their home. I felt like I could not take another footstep until I came up with an answer. I sat under the tree thinking that I had no choice but to go back to the country, yet I knew my mother and family would never believe me. They would laugh at me. Plus I would have no job in the country. With the heat from the sun and confusion around me, my head began to pain me. I started to pray to God for a way out. I stood up and continued my painful walk alone.

By now all of the church members had already gone home, and I was on the street with the midday sun on my back. My shoes were not helping me either, and my corns were burning my toes. Just when I felt empty and alone, there was a ray of hope for me. I heard my name being called from a distance. When I looked to see who it was, I saw no one, so I kept walking. My name was called again. This time I stood to the side of the road and looked behind me and thoroughly down both sides of the road. I finally saw someone waving from a porch. She was a coworker, the lady who gave me lunch every day at work. All the pain left me from my head and my toes.

I walked over to the porch and told my friend Jen that things were not going well at the pastor's home and that I knew they would want me to leave. She told me I could stay with her. Since she was visiting at a friend's house, she told her friend that she was leaving.

I did not tell her what George had done to me especially once she started speaking very highly of him saying, "Oh, he is a good Christian guy. I have known him since he was a young boy. He has never been into any trouble. The only sad thing I know of him is that their father beat his mother in front of them. It is good to see him come to be a preacher."

I continued my silence as she went on talking about him. I began to understand what he meant when he said that no one would believe me if I told what had been done to me.

I walked with Jen until we were at the gate of the pastor's home.

"Would you like me to come inside," she offered, "And help you pack your things?"

"No, I can take care of it."

We said goodbye, and she continued on to her home about five houses away. Walking up the stairs with my knees shaking, not knowing what to expect, I knew it would be unfavorable. I opened the door and went in; they were just finishing their lunch.

When the pastor heard me, he turned and said, "Miss Ruth, I have to talk to you now." I sat down, and both the pastor and his wife came over. She had a big smile on her face.

"I know you are not the right person for George. He confided in me, and I have to look out for his interests," said the pastor. "You were about to say things about him to my wife, but you changed your mind, and I let him know what my wife said. I cannot have you in my home any longer. He is the reason why you are here, and he does not wish to see you any longer. He will be up to the country to hand you back to your mother."

"Thank you for allowing me to stay in your home," I stood before continuing. "But I will be leaving as soon as I pack my things."

They shared surprised looks especially since no bus traveled to the country on a Sunday. I went to the bedroom and started packing my things. My bedroom door opened, and the wife came in with a forced smile as if she cared for me. All she wanted was to inquire so as to gossip. "So, where are you going to stay?" she asked.

Smiling just as she did to me, I replied, "Where there is a will, there is a way."

My answer must have hit her like a ton of bricks because she ran out of the room. I continued my packing and then walked out carrying my two bags. I was still dressed in my church attire and did not even change my shoes that were burning my toes. I could sense that the pastor's wife was looking through the window to see what direction I headed, so I walked the long way around out of sight.

While walking to my new home, I felt like a drifter. A nobody. I used to be teased a lot because of my figure, and I began to feel depressed because of all that was said about me. I felt like a thin country girl that should return to the countryside. I walked with my head down, ashamed to look people in their faces, and almost walked past my new home.

My friend and her children were out on their porch waiting. I entered her home; she had a meal prepared as her way of welcoming me. It was the first time I ate lunch on Sunday without being told that I should leave half of it for my supper. The children were ages five and three, and they seemed glad to have me living with them.

On Monday morning, Jen and I got the children ready for school and nursery. When it was time to leave for work, I told her that I did not want the pastor and his wife to see me on the way to work because I did not want them to know of my whereabouts. She said, "We can take a shorter route. I will show you the way."

The shorter route saved us a lot of time. We walked through an open field, and then we jumped over some long chains that tied the cows so that they could graze in a wide area. I felt lifted in spirit and had a bit of excitement as I imitated my friend's every move. She looked back at me and said softly, "We must be careful when passing this bull. Tread softly. I think it is sleeping."

We did not have to jump over the bull's chain because it was not in our way. I knew that I must check the ground before I placed my feet, and suddenly I heard a sort of squashing noise in front of me. My friend's foot was in a big heap of fresh cow's dung!

"Oh no! Oh no! What did I do?" Jen began screaming. The big black bull jumped up and we ran as fast as we could all the way to work. When we got there, we noticed that her shoes were ruined by that mishap. Thankfully, she always kept a spare pair of shoes at her machine, a flat shoe that helped her to work faster.

Our work building had one large galvanized door that slid from one side to the other when it was time to enter. After the signal went off, I proceeded to my machine, cleaned it so as to make it dust free, and began working on the sewing assignment given to me for that day. In our clothing factory, each person was assigned one task that was done repeatedly for the entire shift. On this day, my task was sewing both sides of a shirt and passing it over to my friend to be completed. My supervisor gave me some verbal instructions to confirm that I had the knowledge of what the company required as the finished product. I gave her the assurance that I understood the instructions.

I got through the first bundle of shirts quickly, but then my emotions triggered and flashbacks about being raped started. The building did not have any windows, just the large door that was closed most of the time. I began to sweat profusely and was not aware that the perspiration was seeping through my top. I failed to focus on my task, and Jen noticed. She did not want to embarrass me, so she asked me to go to the washroom and told me that she would meet me there. We were not allowed to talk while we worked. I stood up and went to the washroom, but my friend could not leave at the same time with me, or my supervisor would ask questions.

A little later my friend came to the washroom and asked me if I was sick because my top was wet and half of the bundle that I sent to her was incomplete. She continued saying, "I hid them under my work so no one will see. I will stay in at lunchtime to help you finish them. This is work that you have done before, and you did it well. What is going on?"

I told her that I was just having a bad day with all that took place on Sunday. She did not know that my boyfriend was angry at me, and when she said she would contact him to tell him where I was staying, I became fearful and anxious. My stomach tightened and I felt nauseated. I feared that George might tell her that she should turn me out of her home.

After my friend left the washroom, I heard another knock on the washroom door. It was my supervisor checking in on me because I was in the washroom for longer than she thought I should be. We were closely watched by our supervisor. We were no longer our own when our feet stepped into that building; we belonged to the boss and had to be aware of production and company time. When my supervisor left the washroom, she must have advised the business owner that I was in the washroom for a long time.

Next thing I knew, the business owner walked into the female washroom, and I began to scream and told him to get out. He ran out. Both the supervisor and the business owner were well aware of the fact that I knew my human rights, and this made them uncomfortable.

I washed my face and walked back to my work station. The boss' office was facing us; he was sitting looking through a big glass window staring at me. I looked him in the face and continued my work.

I began to pray about the meeting my friend and the preacher were going to have. I was afraid he would tell her not to have me at her home, but I was determined to stay in town and work.

On our return home from work, Jen and I ate supper. At eight o'clock she picked up the house keys and said, "I am going to see your boyfriend. Are you coming?"

"Oh no, I will stay with the children" I replied.

With her keys and flashlight in hand she walked out the door. I gave the children some toys to play with and went to the washroom to pray. Twenty minutes later, there was a sound of keys turning in the door. We ran to the door to open it. I was very nervous, but outwardly displayed calm.

"Why are you back so soon?"

"That was a walk in vain because he is not home and no one is there."

My heart returned to its regular pace, and I thanked God.

The next day our boss asked everyone to work overtime, and he gave us a cup of free coffee along with an additional dime added to each dollar we usually made. All the ladies began to murmur amongst themselves, but no one spoke out. I stood up and said that I did not want to drink coffee and that I had church at night. Then everyone found their voice. My friend asked, "Who will look after my children?" Everyone was now talking as I took my seat.

A small voice began to speak within me saying, "This is your way out." I found myself asking myself, "This is my way out of what?" Then I realized my friend would stay if I stayed on to work, and she would not have the time to go and see George. It was like a clear moment of inspiration.

I then stood up and said to the boss that I could work, but on church nights I couldn't stay. He said, "That is fine. Thank you." The others did not say anything and the meeting was over.

The atmosphere became filled with peace. As the ladies saw I was willing to work, they all agreed to work as well. They could not understand why I was not afraid of the boss as they were. From the first day of the job, I let my boss know that I was a Christian and what I stood for.

4

Testings

One day my boss came to test me. He sat at my machine and began talking to me. All of a sudden, his hand was on my leg. I immediately shouted and told him that his actions were abhorrent and inappropriate. Everyone began to look around, and he quickly stood up and proceeded to his office. That was both the first and the last time he made such advances towards me. Some of the ladies allowed it because they saw it as a means of keeping their job. What was foremost in my mind was the need to honor God and keep my salvation.

Later on he called me into his office. He pointed to the chair that faced his desk and invited me to sit. I sat and then he said, "You are a troublemaker and the ladies look up to you. I will pay you more to stay on late, but don't let anyone know of it." I was a leader and did not know the influence I had on those around me. I agreed to stay and walked out of the office. I felt as though I was betraying the others, but then I realized that if they had resisted his advances and not given in, they too would have had an opinion that mattered. I still did not work every night, and I worked the regular hours on the nights of prayer meetings. This made a profound statement that confirmed the importance of God in my life.

On Sunday morning, I had to attend the church. I did not go for adult Sunday school because I knew who was teaching. After what he did to me in his home, I could not bear to see him. I repeatedly experienced horror as I envisioned his blood-red eyes. I intentionally arrived when the service was in progress and everyone was singing joyfully.

I looked towards the front of the church because one could tell who was preaching because that person always sat next to the pastor. Seated next to the pastor was the young pastor who told me he loved me so much. I saw them clearly from where I sat, and I observed when the pastor leaned over and whispered into his ear. I knew that they were not expecting to see me at church. George nodded his head in agreement with what the pastor was saying.

At the end of the worship service, the pastor began to preach. George then came down and sat at the front. I felt that the pastor decided to adjust the printed agenda and use the opportunity to preach because I was present. I felt as though I was in the wrong place. As soon as the pastor uttered his first sentence, I took my Bible and went out. I sat down in the children's nursery until I heard the last song at the end of the service. I hurried out of the nursery so that I would not have any conversations with anyone and to avoid being asked my new address.

After lunch my friend and I went to the beach with the children. I enjoyed myself and felt wonderful because of the soothing effect of the waves and the salt water. That was such a contrast to what took place next.

On our way back to the beach, I felt dizzy. I thought that it was from being hit by the waves, so I did not pay any attention to how I felt. I thought to myself that after a good night's rest, I would be fine. On Monday morning I awoke and smelled food being cooked and the sound of pots and pans in the kitchen as my friend cooked lunch for work. I went to the kitchen to see what she was cooking. As I got closer, my mouth became full of phlegm. She was cooking rice with chicken. As I made my way to the bathroom, the dizzy feeling came back.

Returning to my room, I asked myself, "What is wrong with me?" My mind went back to the days at the river and hearing the older ladies talk about not being able to smell different things when they were with child. My heart began to race. It couldn't be. I thought that I would wait to see if there was any change in my monthly cycle.

Beginning that morning, I had great difficulty in consuming breakfast and sometimes even lunch. I told my friend that I would be working through lunch hour to make more money. She told me that the food would be there for me. At two o'clock, I went to the lunch room and threw the food away. Thank goodness for green mangoes, which I ate for lunch to settle my stomach. I also ate a piece of cake and later drank some water. I kept the fact that a baby was growing inside of me a secret. The cravings I had for mangoes led me to hide mangoes under my bed so that I could consume them with salt and pepper.

The day my monthly cycle should have started, I spotted a bit. I told my friend that I would be going to church that night. I hurried home, put my bag down, and went to see George. I decided not to go into his house. When I arrived, no one was at home, and the door had a padlock on the outside. I sat on the stairs, and shortly afterwards, I heard some footsteps coming towards me. I stood up.

Apparently shocked at my presence, George shouted, "What are you doing here?"

I was frightened and began to mumble, and then finally said, "I want to speak with you about something important."

"I don't want to hear what you have to say," he spat out with anger. "Get out of my yard immediately."

Realizing he wouldn't listen to me, I shouted, "I am pregnant because of what you did to me!"

George's eyes opened wide, and he nervously looked around at the neighbors while trying to locate his keys. He opened the door. "Please, come in."

"I will not," I adamantly declared. "Not after last time."

"Okay, I'll talk with you outside. Just keep your voice down."

"You're the one who started all the shouting."

We sat down outside. George wanted to know if I was sure of being pregnant and then asked where I was living. He dropped his head to his hands, overwhelmed by what I had said, and remained in that position for quite a while. He then lifted his head and stated, "I'll have to marry you. Come back tomorrow, and we will discuss this further. My sisters will be home soon, and I do not want them to know about this."

"Okay." I stood up and left.

On my way back to my friend's home, I had mixed feelings. I was relieved that he did not deny what was happening in my body, but was sad that I would have to get married to cover up for what he had done to me. The thought of joining myself with this wolf made my skin crawl. I wished that I had someone to talk to who would believe and understand me, but I did not know who to trust.

My taste buds and sense of smell all changed. I could no longer eat my friend's food; dry bread was like candy to me. Mangoes were in season, and the younger the mango and the more sour it was, the better – it was like food from heaven. I did not notice that I was losing weight, I had always been skinny, but people began to ask me why I was looking so pale and thin.

The next day at work, I did not tell anyone that I was leaving early. As soon as it was five o'clock, I left the factory. I knew I had to go and speak with George. I went home and changed from my work clothes, and then I began the painful steps towards my preacher boyfriend's home. He had said that he would be home early from work so we could talk before his sisters got home. I remembered what he had done to me before when I was alone, so I decided not to enter the house when I got there. As I got closer to his house, my heart began to pump faster and faster. Turning the corner to his street, I could see his house at the end of the road and him sitting on the steps waiting for me. When he saw me approaching, he went inside.

I walked up to the front door, knocked, then turned around, and went down to the lower step to sit. He shouted from inside for me to come in, but I decided not to move from where I was. When he realized that I was not coming inside, he pushed his head outside and tried to persuade me to come in. I held my ground until he came outside to me.

"Try and talk very quietly," he admonished. "I don't want my nosey neighbor to hear. I know she always eavesdrops in the bushes."

He never asked me how I felt or what I thought. He took it upon himself to order me around by telling me how this would bring his good name down and how this is what everyone was trying to protect him from and how what they had said had finally happened. He continued to tell me that I had nothing to offer since I was a country girl. He told me that I was a liability not an asset. I could not get a word in edgewise; he was just going on and on.

Then George pulled a brown paper bag from his pocket and handed it to me.

"What's in this?" I asked.

"The guys from the tailor shop talk about this stuff that they buy in the drugstore to give to the girlfriend when she gets pregnant. They told me that this will kill the child. First, drink the whole bottle all at once, which will do the trick."

I opened the bottle and smelled the contents. It smelled like pesticide. I closed the bottle. "I can do no such thing."

"Then we will have to get married quickly. I will go up and see your father in the country on the weekend and tell him that I am going to marry you."

My father had never talked to him. Every time George sent a message to my father telling him he would like to meet him, my father would not show up. I think my dad sensed something only a man could sense, but never told me anything. The days went by so fast, and then I found myself packing some things to go up to the country. Jen wanted to send her daughter with me to use as her eyes and ears since Jen herself could not be present. I told her not this time but I promised that I would take her next time. I said goodbye and went to the bus stop where the preacher was waiting for me.

George and I climbed on to a big bus painted blue with a red stripe. On the roof of the bus, the market ladies placed their baskets of fruit or whatever they had brought from the countryside to town. On the way back home, the same baskets would be filled with fish and other things not available where the ladies lived. The bus, made to carry about fifty people, was crowded with over one hundred people. Some people were even hanging on the outside of the bus.

Because I was sitting in the middle of some big, loud-mouthed market ladies, George did not have the opportunity to talk to me on the way there. Whenever the bus turned a deep corner, my body usually felt the crushing effects caused by sitting next to oversized ladies. This time, I sat on a seat meant for two, but instead of sitting on the wooden bench seat, I rested on the hips of two large ladies to the left and right of me. With thousands of thoughts running through my mind, I found comfort between the well-cushioned ladies. When the bus fell into pot holes, it did not affect me. I felt as though I was in a cradle, and I fell into a deep dream-filled sleep.

I dreamt about my mother and me. I told her of all that happened with the preacher, and she gave me a big hug telling me everything would be okay. She also told me not to marry him. Just then I found myself falling onto the hard wooden bench. The bus had stopped to let one of the ladies off, and there was a big space soon filled by someone else. Looking around, my eyes connected with George and I realized I had been dreaming. Sleeping had become a doorway for me to leave my painful life. I controlled some of my dreams and became a star in my world. Dreams were a place where no one could hurt me, and I could be whoever I wanted to be.

Reality set in once more, and I began to smell the fish and sweat along with the horrible smell of whisky breath coming from an old man. I learned my lesson well on previous trips – Never sit next to the men on the bus because many of them can drink a lot and soil their clothes. When the bus went around the corner, the urine ran to one side of the bus.

I had one more mile to go before reaching my street. My stop was first, and then the preacher had to travel for another ten minutes before reaching his cousin's house. By this time most of the people had reached their destination. Without an oversized market lady blocking my view,

I could see through the window of the bus. I watched the waves rolling to the shore and back again. Higher up, I saw some fishing boats getting ready to come ashore. People were waiting on the shore to pull the boats in, and ladies were standing holding their plates and baskets to buy fresh fish. I could remember those days from when I was living in the country. The sea shell was blown, which meant the fishing boat had just come to shore.

There was always something interesting to see when travelling on the bus. Most of the houses were very close to the road, and the people got accustomed to the buses passing by. One lady was taking a bath at the side of her house, wearing only her birthday suit! A little further along a man was running after a black dog. The dog had a large piece of meat in its mouth. There were a few seconds to capture a bit of everything.

The bus stopped to let someone off, and some of the guys that I knew from my village came to speak with me. They were easy-going, not rude like other street boys. George could not hear what they were saying to me, so he called out to me. I pretended not to hear him. The bus drove off, and I still did not answer him. When my stop came, I shouted to the bus driver as everyone does, "Leave one here." I paid the driver and did not look back.

A voice behind me said, "Who were those guys? Are they interested in you?" I turned around and asked George to repeat what he said, and he did.

"Oh, I wonder which one of them got me pregnant!"

George was silent for a moment. "Don't say anything about being pregnant. I'll handle everything," he ordered. "Just talk only of our wedding."

As I began to walk into the yard, memories of my dog Ginger came back to me. She would have been there greeting me as I entered the yard, except my mom got rid of her the same day I moved to town to work. She sold Ginger to an old man for five dollars, and she died of starvation shortly afterwards. Sometimes the simple things in our lives can mean so much to us.

Before we entered the yard, the preacher pulled me behind him and walked in front of me. My mother was sitting in front of the main door of the house assigning duties so each would know who must go to the standpipe for water and who must go sweep the yard. George walked up to her and gave her a hug. I said good afternoon, but she became completely caught up with speaking to her soon-to-be son-in-law.

I went to change in the little bedroom that my mom and dad shared. My younger sisters and brothers came in to see what I had brought for them. I took out a plastic bag with cakes and gave it to the eldest. They all ran out of the room happy as they went to eat the cakes. I stumbled over my clothing on the ground. In the tiny bedroom I was now alone. My father was not at home, and we did not know if he would show up. My mother and her perfect soon-to-be son-in-law were still chatting.

It was getting dark when my father appeared. He was shocked to see that the man he had been avoiding was at his home. George did not waste any time.

"Good afternoon. I'm here to tell you that I'd like to marry your daughter."

"Wait a while. I'll be back to speak with you." My father then disappeared into the house. He returned with a pen and a notebook and asked, "When is the wedding?" I myself did not know the date.

"December," replied the preacher and he gave a specific day.

"That is next month and it is only now that you are telling me this?"

With quick thinking and determination to always be right, George was ready to answer all the questions my father asked. The preacher told my father, "I came here on two occasions and you never showed up." That was true because my father had stood us up twice, but George was not going to ask for my hand in marriage at those times. He had told me he just wanted to know what kind of man my father was.

"I want to inquire about you before meeting with you," said my father as he closed the notebook. "I know what men are like. I am a man." He then disappeared out of the yard. It was his last visit home for the day.

"See you tomorrow," George told my mother as he left for his cousin's home.

I turned to my brother and asked when he last saw Niasa, my best friend.

"Niasa is not living at home anymore," he said. "She ran away because of a guy and is now staying at her grandmother's home."

At her grandmother's home, she had her freedom with no set boundaries. Her grandmother was very old and could not manage her. I was shocked at the news and did not know how to tell her mother that I was going to get married, but I had to because she was often nice to me. All mothers wish to know when their daughters are getting married. At that time, Niasa's mother did not have that hope because in my neighborhood a guy would not commit if he got things easily. If the guy had taken what was not his by force like the preacher did, he may have married her.

As I looked around, a lot of changes were visible at home and in the village. A heap made up of a mixture of both stone and sand occupied the space that used to be my beautiful flower garden. My parents were about to build a brick house. In the village, most of the girls that I knew had moved away to other villages.

When the time came to sleep, the usual fighting began for my father's old pants and shirts to sleep in. The next step was a fight for the best spot to rest our weary bones. No one wanted to sleep next to the door. I myself was afraid to sleep there. Often times we would wake up in the middle of the night and see the front door wide open. When I tried to turn, my feet would kick it open. The lock was not good, and we would sometimes tie the door closed with a string. Since it was totally dark both inside and outside, I crawled under the table to sleep. The only light came from a lamp in the tiny bedroom with my mom. She would blow it out before she went to sleep.

Lying under the table in a fetal position in my parent's house, I began to think of how my life was going and what it would be like to get married. In the countryside, the days had been lovely. Life and raw nature were all around. I had played in the fields while my sheep were grazing, and then would hear the trilling reminder that the night was coming. I would stop for the moment and then return back to what I was doing. Now I could not think of any happy thoughts because I knew who I was going to marry.

I began to listen to the crickets making noises outside. Then I heard the sound of running water. We did not have any faucets in our yard or in the house, so I knew it was one of my younger brothers wetting the bed. He went to bed without any pants, so he sprayed the one sleeping closest to him. He was still fast asleep. Not long after, I heard movements in the dark. Someone was looking for a dry spot to sleep. I knew the feeling quite well.

I can remember sleeping close to one of my sisters who would wet her bed every night. In the morning I would be in her spot because she would roll me over, take my dry spot, and tell my mom I was the one who wet the bed. My mom would make us wash the bedding and scrub the floor. One night I waited for my sister as she tried to pull me onto the wet spot. I held my ground. I was the one who put her to the test before our mom. She still tried to lie her way out of the situation, saying that it was not her and that I was the one who had rolled her over into the wet. I told my mom to feel her underwear and then feel mine. My sister ran away in guilt.

As I lay under the table remembering those days, I drifted off to sleep. The next day was Sunday, and I was the first to wake up. I went outside and sat on a bench, but it was still a bit chilly as the sun was not up as yet. One by one the others came out. I went down to the kitchen and opened the door and let the goat and sheep out. I began to clean the mess that they had made that night. I could not do anything about the smell; there were puddles of animal urine on the dirt floor. I went outside and gathered some dry sand to cover the puddles up. I began to clean the kitchen the best I could; I did not wait for my mom to tell me what to do. I knew what must be done if I wanted to attend church that Sunday morning. The mother goat and the sheep were tied up to the side fence of the yard. They stood on their back legs to reach the branches that were hanging over from the neighbor's yard as the young lambs and goats ran around making mischief.

Next, I went up to the house and gathered all of the urine soaked bedding. I placed them in a large laundry tub and went back into the house. When I returned, one of the kid goats was eating the wash soap. We called him Joey – he was a trouble maker. When you were not looking, he would sneak up behind you and adopt the posture of a goat that was ready for a fight. If you were sitting on a stone in the yard, he would creep up behind you and nibble on your ears. I took the soap from Joey, placed it in the laundry tub, and then placed the tub on my head to begin walking to the river. I heard tiny steps behind me, and when I turned around, I saw Joey. I called one of my little brothers to come and get Joey.

The sun was not high enough to take the chill out of the river water, so I took a deep breath as I placed one foot in front of the other. Entering the chilly water of the river, only one lady and I were at the riverside. After washing the bedding, I took a bath and then walked home to scrub the floor where all the wet spots were to be found. I took the tub that I filled with water and a piece of coconut shell for a brush. I decided to scrub the whole floor. That morning we had boiled green bananas and salt fish for breakfast. I did not eat the salt fish, only a bit of green banana, and drank some herbal tea.

My mom was now getting ready for church. I had to wait in order to use the one bedroom we had in the house. She told my sister to cook and what she must buy in the village so as to prepare the lunch. The preacher's relatives attended the church that my mother attended, and I expected to see them that day. My mom always left early for church. She normally went to the home of an elderly lady with arthritis pain to help her get dressed. Her granddaughter was just five years old and needed help too. We all went to the same church so it was a pleasure for my mother to help her.

Once my mother left, I was able to have the bedroom all to myself. I combed my hair, and then I took out my best dress which we called our Sunday best. It was a long blue dress with a very wide round collar that sat on my shoulders. At the end of the collar was a black frill all around. The dress touched the floor until I put my high-heeled black shoes on. I knew my hairstyle was very nice. I then looked down in front of me and observed that my upper body, being well developed, filled out the top of the dress. I could not see the back of the dress because we did not have a large mirror, only a small piece that enabled me to see my face.

After placing my offering in the pages of my Bible since I didn't have a purse, I started the long walk from my home to the church. On my way, I met my mom and the older lady that my mom went to help. We reached the crossing where one could take the back road, which was shorter, or walk on the main road. I knew that I was dressed for the red carpet and wanted everyone to see me, so I decided to take the main street while my mom and the older lady took the back street.

As I past the people on the street they all complimented me on my dress. One lady called me into her yard and began to warn me.

"My child, I look at you growing up and how you kept yourself from getting into trouble. Now you are a fine young lady. Keep it up and don't let any man touch you or you know you will end up like some of my daughters. They never listened to me."

I thanked her for her advice and then said, "I'm getting married soon."

She got up from the big stone she was sitting on to give me a hug. "I am so glad for you! These girls I have here will never give me that joy. When I talk to them they speak disrespectfully to me." Then, as was a custom among some of the elders, she spat in the air believing that she was able to curse them by that action.

I told her I would see her again, and I went on my way. When I passed by the supermarket with its large glass windows, I looked at my entire reflection in the glass. From top to bottom, back to front, I said to myself, "Girl, you are looking good. Who says the country girl can't be pretty?"

Next I came to the bridge where the young guys always hang out. You can always find the good, the bad, and the ugly sitting on a wall next to the bridge. I knew they were troublesome, so I wore an expression on my face which carried the message to "keep your distance." They always tried to make a joke, and if they saw the slightest response, they interpreted it as permission to get close. They tried to touch you and walk with you, whispering foolish words in your ears. I had seen it happen over and over. So I had my message written on my face as they joked as a way to get me to smile. I clenched my teeth together and cast my mind elsewhere as I kept my determination not to laugh because some of their jokes were silly enough to make one laugh. I felt as though I was never going to step out of their sight! I was walking in heels and had to shorten my steps plus my long dress proved to be an additional hindrance. I began to perspire in the hot sun, and I could feel perspiration running down my back. Sweat was all over my face.

When I reached the church, I stopped at the standpipe to wash my face before entering the building. We were early, and my mom and some of the older folks were sitting and talking while they waited. Apparently, she had already given them the news of the intended marriage because they all gave me a big smile and referred to me as their daughter when I said good morning. I took a window seat to get some fresh air.

Minutes later, a large crowd entered. It was the family of the preacher. He entered last after standing outside drying his face with a large handkerchief. Some of the girls came and sat with me as we whispered to each other.

Every Sunday morning was communion. Only those that were baptized and/or members of that church could partake. Those who were participating sat in the front in a circle while visitors and other members of the family who were not saved sat at the back. For a while, I sat in the back to chat with the girls. Then, just before the service began, I went and sat in one of the front pews.

In this particular church, women were not allowed to speak. They were only allowed to say "amen" now and again.

To commence the Sunday morning service, the elder stood and began to pray. After he finished, every person in the church would say a prayer. Sometimes one brother would pray for half an hour. Regular church attendees knew what he was going to say when he started. He started with

"O Lord, you know," and all heads would bow and snoring could be heard coming from all around. After the prayers, communion was served.

I always tried to sit up front to receive the cup first. There was only one large cup, and everyone had to drink from it. Some of the older people did not have teeth, just gums; and those who had a few teeth did not practice good hygiene. I'm sure God would not be mad with me for using my brain. In the days when Jesus was on earth, I imagine that some of the diseases we are faced with today did not exist, and if they had, Jesus blessed the communion, which was truly a blessed communion.

Our communion was not grape juice, but strong wine; those who loved their liquor took a big gulp. No matter how small a sip I took, the wine always put me fast asleep. The sun beat down outside on the galvanized roof, and the church became very hot with no fans in the unsealed room. The heat, combined with the strong wine, made me very sleepy, and I began to snore with the rest. The lady next to me touched me. If you were to ask me what the preacher said, I wouldn't be able to tell you. I knew for sure that I had a good sleep, and so did many others.

After church we went around shaking hands with everyone. I walked home with a large group of people from church, so George did not get to talk privately with me. On our way home, he complained to everyone of not being asked to come and sit in the front. Then he said, "I am a Christian and a preacher, and no one even called upon me to pray."

Someone tried to explain to George that it was the custom of the church. All the "holier than thou" sat to the front as though they were so clean, leaving all the unclean in the back. In my opinion, this should not have been, and I decided to talk with the elder about that.

George spoke so much on our way home that his saliva gathered at the corner of his mouth. His cousin and I started laughing. He assumed we were just talking girl talk, but the reason why I was laughing was because she kept saying I must go and kiss the saliva away. I had no feelings for him after what he had done to me, but I did not tell his cousin anything about our relationship. I was fearful of her telling the others and my having a bigger problem. We all walked from Georgetown until we reached my village. Someone in the crowd shouted, "Peppervillage!"

"Oh yes, Peppervillage is my stop," I said.

"I'll come to see you later," called George to me. "Don't eat too many peppers."

I did not look back; I kept my head straight on to my own Peppervillage. The village name came from the everyday confusion (fighting). When I was living close to the seaside, the people called the area Crab Island because of all the sea crabs and other big crabs that lived in and around the yards. The children of another village used to tease us and say, "Go back to Crab Island," when we all met at the standpipe. Their taunting usually caused a village fight – my village against the other village.

Although we did not have much to eat at the time, I had been much happier living on Crab Island. (The real name is Landley Park.) Nine coconut trees were in the yard with a row planted close to the seaside. The sea always gave us surprises. I can remember one day we had nothing to eat, so, to occupy our time, my sister and I went for a walk on the beach. We saw some small packages on the sand; we began gathering them up and then opened one, just to find it was food for us. It was popcorn covered in a brown sugar liquid; it also had small toys in the box. My sister and I gathered as much as we could carry, then ran home to show the others. My eldest sister read the box that said Cracker Jacks®. The boxes had come from a ship that was overloaded. We often found all sorts of things on the beach, but that day it was like manna from Heaven.

Speaking about manna from Heaven, I can remember that dreadful day when people from Sandy Bay found barrels on the beach. Everyone went down to see what it was. They all opened the barrels and began to drink what it contained. They said that God had sent Jack Iron, which means rum, from Heaven. Mothers even gave it to their young ones, and everyone in the village partook. Not long afterwards people began to drop like flies; there was not enough room in the morgue to contain the bodies. People of all ages, hundreds of people, died, and those who survived became blind. After someone from another village went up to see what was killing the people of the village, they quickly told the remaining people not to partake of the fluid because it was aircraft fuel. Some were still partaking, believing that those who warned us wanted to trick us and take it for themselves.

Yes, good old Crab Island, you never felt the heat of the sun and where every sea wave is different and speaks to you as they splash against the stones or the sand. The rolling of the sea waves rocked us to sleep at night.

One day my mother got the news that people were taking government land to use to build houses. She ran over to the area with four large sticks in her hand. I was one step behind her all the way. As we got close, we saw two women fighting for the best spot of land. My mother pulled my hand as we passed them. She took the four sticks and made a line as she marked out her plot of land. My father, who was a carpenter, built a tiny shack on it just to let people know that the land had been taken. We also planted different crops there.

Then the day came when my mom turned our world around. She began to pack everything in old sheets and placed them on our heads. She said to us, "We are moving to Peppervillage. I hear that your father is sleeping there in the house with all kinds of women."

I ran down to the second floor and began to cry. I cried not for what my mother said about my father, but because we had to move to that small shack. One side of the shack did not have any flooring.

My mom packed us up like donkeys, and we walked through the streets with heavy loads on our heads. I was so ashamed when I met my friends in the street. We asked her to do the moving in the night, but she did not pay us any mind.

That night we all sat up and slept, all nine children. My three eldest sisters said they were not coming; they stayed in the large brick house. They each took a bedroom for themselves and had the entire house for themselves.

I cried myself to sleep that night; no one said a word to one another.

There was no lamp lit. That was my exodus from Crab Island (Landley Park) to Peppervillage.

Walking away from the preacher as he continued to talk to his cousins, I thought to myself, "Look at what I'm going to live with." My mother had survived a life of abuse, so maybe I could too. On the other hand, I loved the attention I was getting from people who heard that I was about to be married.

As I entered our yard, everyone was sitting under a tree eating lunch. My younger sister said to me, "Go and get your food before changing or else they will eat it all." She was talking about my younger brothers and sisters. There was never enough to make us all feel full.

I went down to the kitchen and rolled up my dress not wanting any black from the smoke to touch my beautiful gown. I spotted a plate with a big pot cover over it. Removing the cover, I saw that someone had removed the better part of the food. I could see where they hurriedly grabbed the meat, which was completely gone, and just a handful of rice remained scattered on the plate. I took the rest of it and went up to change.

After I changed, I picked a lemon from behind the kitchen to make lemon juice. My youngest sister began scolding me saying that the sugar was for breakfast. She forgot or did not care to find out who was sending money each weekend to buy food. She got her strength from my mom; she was my mother's favorite. She was perfect in my mother's eyes. Ignoring my sister, I took my plate and lemon juice to the back of the kitchen. My youngest brother was walking close behind me, and I knew he wanted some of my juice. After sharing with him, we sat there in silence, strengthening the bond we once shared.

When he was born, mother immediately put him in my arms for me to take care of night and day, as I had done with the others. But he was different; maybe it was because he was the last baby of the family to be born alive. He was now three years old and would always be my baby brother, close to my heart. We sat there watching our neighbor with her children playing cricket. Her family was large enough to have two sons that played against each other.

My brothers and sisters went to the river for a bath before Sunday school. I decided not to go. I had the feeling that I would run into the preacher at the river. Not long after they left, my siblings came back running and shouting, "A message for you! A message for you!"

"What is the message? Who is it from?" I asked them.

"Your boyfriend."

"The one you are going to marry."

Putting my hands in the air, I said, "Stop, every one of you." Then I pointed to one of my brothers and asked him, "What is going on?"

"The guy you are, you know, the one you are going to, you know, he said he is coming over now. He is going to get dressed. You must wait for him."

"Okay, everyone," I said, "Get ready so we can all go to Sunday school together."

They scrambled off to find clothes to put on. Some found socks but could not find shoes. We all pitched in to help each other dress. My mom, who was resting in the bedroom, shouted, "I can't wait until you are all gone out of the yard!" Sometimes the noise of eleven children was totally unbearable to her and she would hit us randomly in anger.

Everyone was ready except one of my smaller brothers, who could only find one shoe. We did a quick search of the small house, but didn't find his shoe. Then I remembered Joey, the goat kid, who loved to take things in his mouth and run behind the kitchen. Walking towards the kitchen with my crying brother next to me, I reassured him that he would get to go with us. Each of my siblings had only one pair of shoes and needed the shoes for walking. No extra pairs were around anywhere. As we walked behind the kitchen, we spotted the shoe next to the fence pole. I told my brother to go wash his face while I cleaned off the sand from the shoe. Finally, with everyone ready, we all said goodbye to mom. As we walked out of the yard, one of my brothers asked if I would wait for my boyfriend; I told him George would meet us on the way.

We were about to turn the first corner when we heard a crowd behind us shouting, "Wait for us! Wait for us!" It was George and his cousins. We all laughed and joked around as we walked on the back street to get away from the hot sun. It was a dirt road with large trees shading our walk. Some of the children tried to reach for the hanging branches to see who was taller. Since the preacher loved being the center of attention, he made it a point to show the children how far he could reach the tree limbs that were hanging towards the road.

George was six foot, two inches tall and very slim with an afro with a patch of grey hair to the front, close to his right temple. He had a pug nose with very large thick lips and a small goatee beard. Because he was tall and dark, he always talked about how handsome he was. As the saying goes, beauty is in the eyes of the beholder. He loved to look at himself in the mirror, so I can't blame him for seeing himself as the most handsome man God ever made.

We reached a shortcut but decided not to take it because the smaller children would have to jump on stones to get across the river. We headed for the bridge, which took us ten extra minutes to reach the church. Just before we entered the church building, George suggested we go for a walk because we were too big for children's Sunday school. We went walking through Georgetown.

The sun was still strong at four in the afternoon, and we were craving a drink of water. Then we heard the sound of bells ringing getting closer to us. A man was riding a cart selling snow cones and shouting, "Come and get it! Come and get it." The man asked what color we wanted, and George asked for an orange and a green. I asked the man to give me a red, but George looked at me sternly. The first cone was green, and I realized that one belonged to George. After the man handed me the red one, the preacher quickly took it away from me and began to eat it. He handed the money to the man while still holding the two snow cones in his hand as he licked them one after the other. When he was finished licking all of the milk from the red one, he handed it to me. I asked him for a taste of his, but he said, "No, the guy gave you more milk than me."

I stood there watching him placing his large lips over the cone while trying to talk at the same time. I looked at my cone trying to find a place where I thought his mouth had not touched, and I began nibbling sides. He was now on his last bite and began to look at mine. Knowing his intentions, I pretended mine slipped out of my hand, but I was the one who intentionally loosened my hand so it would slip through my palm. I then pretended to be sad about the loss.

We continued walking as he talked of how he wanted the wedding to be. He talked as if he was getting married to himself. His words were only "me" and "I" – "I have to look good…It is my day…No one in my wedding should look better than I." We were now on a long road with tall willow trees on one side. Behind the trees was a cemetery. We stood there and talked for a while. Turning to him I asked, "Who are you getting married to? I heard you speaking about yourself all along with no mention of another person."

Since it was now six-thirty at night and the Sunday night church service began at seven, we walked slowly back to the church. Before we entered the building he whispered to me, "If I don't get a chance to talk with you after church, I'll be on Big Jim's bus in the morning."

Church was about to start, and the song leader was on the pulpit. After a few songs were sung, the person who was going to preach stood behind the song leader as a hint to him that his time was up. Almost every time that this brother preached, his main text was John 3:16, "For God so loved the world…" Knowing word for word what the preacher was going to say my mind began to drift. I began to look at my life.

Just last year I had crossed the threshold to womanhood, and now I was carrying a child within me. At the age of seventeen, after taking care of my siblings, I thought that I would have some time to be a teenager. People often say if life gives you lemons, then make lemonade. My teeth had been on edge all the time from the lemon, and I still could not see the sugar to make it sweet. Because of all the acid that went through my veins, I began getting sudden pains from time to time in my chest.

After church we all departed to our homes, and the fear concerning that night consumed me. The question ran through my mind – will the door kick open tonight or will I hear chains being pulled in the yard? Too often I had been awakened to feel the chill mountain breeze flowing into the room as the darkness that entered engulfed the darkness that was already there. Afraid to move a muscle, I often wondered if there were eyes looking at me in the midst of all the darkness. I decided that if I pretended to be dead and evil spirits were real, they would not harm me. Then the voice of fear would say, "What if you fall asleep? You are risking being carried away." I jumped up and closed the door, still feeling the chilling breeze coming through the space at the door. I tied the string around the nail head twice to keep evil spirits out, thinking that this would be sufficient. The Bible says that people are destroyed for lack of knowledge. In our church that expounded the Word of God, I had seen how the devil used to deprive me of my night's sleep. Hearing the stories the older people told concerning spirits coming to take children out of their homes in the darkest of nights and the demons that were set loose at night looking for souls caused great agony of mind.

In the middle of the night, I heard my mom looking for the potty, but she could not find it in the dark. She lit a candle which cast a shadow of the four chair legs that were turned upside down on the table. All I could see was a large round head floating without a body. I thought the spirit had already entered the house and was now looking at us. The wind blew out the candle, and total darkness fell again. I decided to stay awake to hear if the door would open. The dog next door began to bark, which led to a series of barking throughout the village. The sound of snoring mixed with the sound of the crickets told my brain it was sleeping time.

I was awakened by the donkey braying, and I could see light coming through the cracks in the door. Crawling out from under the table, I came face to face with the floating head. I had not seen my mom place her church hat on one of the chairs legs the night before. In the candlelight, the hat shape appeared to be a floating head. I took the hat and threw it under the table, opened the door, and went outside. There was no clock in the house so I did not know what time it was. The donkey normally brayed around five o'clock and was my signal to get up. Everyone else was still asleep as I began to get ready since the bus would be leaving soon for town.

Then I heard the sound of the bus on the main road. I called to my mom softly to let her know I was leaving, and she grumbled in her sleep. Pushing the door closed quietly behind me, I took up my bag and walked out of the yard. I tried to avoid stepping on the frogs that were making their way back home before the sun came up. On my way to the main road, I met old Joe riding his donkey. A little further down I saw a window open and a pail of water was thrown outside. When I got closer, the stench of urine was present with the wind.

The sound of the bus was getting louder, and I ran towards the main road. I stopped behind a tree to see the name of the bus before stopping it. I did not want to travel on the same bus with the preacher. It was not the bus he was going to take so I began to wave, but the driver did not see me and passed by. Standing outside on the bus was the conductor. I began to call out, "Wait for me!" as I ran behind the bus. The conductor hit the side of the bus to let the driver know that someone was coming. I climbed up into the big wooden bus, sat down, and braced myself for the sharp corners.

I was seated behind the driver, and I looked behind me to see who was in the back rows. There was a pleasant aroma coming from the people. There were no market ladies. This trip carried people who worked in the stores and banks in town along with some school children. A chilly breeze flowed throughout the bus but there were no windows to close, just large open spaces at the side. My small naked arms quickly covered with goose bumps. Looking down on the beach, I thought how even the sea seemed to be asleep with only small waves at the shoreline.

Suddenly, the bus driver applied the brakes, and the entire vehicle jerked. Crossing the street was a large herd of sheep walking slowly followed by cows. Behind the cows was a little old man beating an empty paint can yelling "Hoo, Hooo!" By this time, the sun was peeping over the ocean, and I knew I would soon be in town. Once I reached town, I would have to take a small van to my place of work.

When we reached town, I saw people standing outside at their places of employment waiting for them to open. I was glad to see a van marked Camden Park, which was ten minutes away from town. The van was not yet half full, so the driver drove around looking for more people. I was ten minutes late for work.

After placing my things in the lunchroom, I went to the boss' office. He was seated at his desk. With a big smile on my face, I said, "Good morning! I am sorry to be late. I just came back from the country."

Knowing I was always early, my boss shook his head and said, "Off to your workstation, young lady."

"Thank you, sir."

As I passed Jen on my way to my station, I could tell she wanted to say something. Finally she could not wait any longer. She turned around with a piece of garment pretending to show me something.

"What did the boss say to you?" Jen asked. "He was smiling with you. He just sent someone back home because she was five minutes late."

I told her what he said and then added, "I have good news for you, and I will tell you what it is at break time."

Our first break was at ten o'clock in the morning. I planned to let her know that my boyfriend had asked me to marry him.

5

Knowing Your True Friend

You can know your true friends by their reaction to whatever you share, whether good or bad. Some pretend to be your friend because they are in a better position than you are or because it feels good to know that someone is in the dumps with them.

When the bell rang for break time, I did not move because I was still trying to catch up on my work. The other ladies went outside, but my friend stayed to hear what I had to say. Turning off her machine, she turned to me.

"So, what is the big news?" I was just about to sew up the side of a shirt, so I did not look up at her, but continued to work. She shouted at me, "Well, well, don't leave me hanging!"

Still sewing, I said, "I'm going to get married." I had no intentions of stopping sewing even when she put her hands next to my needle.

"What?!?" she shouted.

Seeing that her fingers were about to be pulled under, I stopped my machine and looked up at her. The lines in her forehead ran deep, and her countenance had fallen. I realized I was now face to face with anger, hurt, pain, and jealousy. Yes, I was looking into the face of the green-eyed monster who was my friend and had wanted to help me. I knew she was angry and jealous because she was never asked to be a bride. Her boyfriend came only on weekends to perform his manly duties and then return to his mother's home. She thought that by having two children with him, he would always be with her.

"Why didn't you tell me before you went out to the country that you were pregnant? Why are you getting married so suddenly?"

I sat there looking at her as jealousy, shock, and anger became dominant within her very being. She never said that she was happy for me or anything like that. I then decided to let her know that I would prefer to continue with our conversation at lunch. I started my machine again and returned to sewing.

At lunch I sat with the group we often ate with, but my friend took both of our lunches and said to the ladies, "I'm going for a walk." She left me there without anything to eat, and I knew that she had a piece of cake in the bag that I wanted. I normally continued working at lunchtime, but I had told her that we could talk at lunch. The ladies looked at each other then back at me trying to elicit a response. I sat there and talked with them. My now angry friend came back before the bell rang. She said nothing to me, and I did not want to upset her any more than she already was. I did not have any money to buy something for my lunch because I had already given her the expense money for the week and the larger portion I had taken to the country.

Everyone returned to work, and the machines began to rumble as did my stomach. I did not have breakfast, nor did I have lunch. Hunger began to take hold of my body, and my hands began to shake. I started feeling dizzy and almost fainted. I made my way to the washroom and threw up, but nothing much came from my stomach. All of a sudden the washroom door slammed open.

Standing in front of me was my friend proclaiming loudly, "I knew it! I knew it! You are pregnant! That is why he is marrying you. Why are you here throwing up?"

With foam still dripping from my mouth, I said, "I'm hungry because I had no lunch. You are free to think whatever you wish."

She left closing the door noisily behind her.

I attempted to drink some water, but it came up as fast as it went down.

I walked back to my machine feeling totally nauseated. I began to pray that the time would pass quickly. I was glad that it was Monday because the boss and the supervisor were very busy and no one was checking our work. I could not ask my friend to help me rip out the sides of a shirt that needed to be sewn over. The day seemed to be longer, and hearing the bell ring was like music to my ears because it indicated that it was time for home.

Everyone had their small group that they walked home with. Our group had ten ladies. As each one reached her home, the group got smaller and smaller, and then it was only my friend and I. We walked in silence. I did not care to start any conversation because I was now both hungry and exhausted. Upon our arrival at home my friend took the lunch bag and went to the back door. She began to shake out the food from the bowl. I knew that was my lunch. The dogs came and feasted with tails wagging in appreciation.

"Kids," she called to her two children who were in my room talking with me, "Let's go for a walk at bum-bum's corner."

I knew she had some friends living there, but she never went there since they had always come to visit. This time she had something to tell. I knew that I was going to be subject of her visit.

I stood in the bedroom peering through a crack in the doorway to see when they left. As soon as the front door closed, I ran to the kitchen and opened the fridge looking for something to eat. I found a bowl of fried chicken, cake, and white rice. I was glad to see the plain rice. The smell of peas made my stomach upset. I began to stuff my mouth as fast as I could. After eating my belly full, I washed my hands. I then proceeded to the bedroom and got ready to go and see the preacher because I did not want him to come and look for me. I knew that he would ask me why I did not take the bus with him. With that thought running through my mind, my stomach began to rumble. I made it to the washroom just in time to throw up all that I had eaten. I began to feel a little bit lightheaded, so I sat on the bed to dress. It was either because the food was too cold or the fact that I had eaten it in such a hurry that caused me to feel ill.

Upon reaching George's home, I knocked then entered the house. His sister was at home with him. When she saw me, she quickly entered the bedroom and slammed the door. He was preparing oatmeal cereal. Pointing to the bedroom door, he whispered to me that his sister was angry with me.

"With me? What for?"

"When I told her that we are getting married, her reply was – so do I have to leave? I told her that this is my home, and I have only one bedroom. I can't have two women living in the same house as it had not worked out when her other sister was here; so I know that it won't be any good for any of us. She will lock me out of my own bedroom; what will she do with you? When I gave her the news she went and saw our father. Maybe she thinks he can change my mind." With the same breath, he pointed the oatmeal-covered spoon at me and asked, "Where were you this morning? I told you to take the bus that I was travelling on."

"Oh, I did not know if that bus had already passed, so I took the first one I saw."

Ignoring my answer, he began to talk about the guys at his workplace whom he had asked to be his groomsmen. He could not leave anyone out, so all ten would be standing next to him. His youngest brother would be his best man. He even had the ladies in mind for my bridesmaids. He had everything planned perfectly as he would like.

"My boss' wife will make you a wedding dress and the bridal cake. I already asked her. You will need to save your money now. Whatever money your parents are giving you, bring to me and I can buy what we need. I cannot look to my father for anything, so we have to make do with what your family provides." Turning to the boiling pot, he began to stir his cereal and then placed the spoon in his mouth. To my disgust, he began slowly pulling the spoon from his mouth, and the cereal formed strands that looked like soft spaghetti. Then he turned his face towards me and asked, "Do you want some porridge?"

"Yes, I would love to have some."

He poured some into a cup and handed it to me. I wanted a spoon but feared he would give me the one he had been licking. The hot porridge went down like rain in a dry desert. He was still talking, but I was not listening. He usually talked and answered himself anyway.

The bedroom door opened and his sister came out. She refused to acknowledge my presence, and I carefully observed her. She went into the washroom and then back to the bedroom slamming both doors as she came and went.

It was now nine-thirty at night. The moon was out in all its brightness and could be seen from the window close to where I was sitting. George poured out some porridge and set it aside for his sister. With the pot in his hand, he walked to the dining table and placed a large phone book down for his table mat. He began to smile from ear to ear, his thick wide lips covered with oatmeal. He said to me, "I love to eat from the pot. It makes me feel full, and I like when the last spoonful is done and the empty pot is looking at me."

I smiled and thought, "You called me a country girl, but I am seeing a bush boy in front of me!"

It was time for me to go home, so he walked me back to my friend's front door. After I placed my hand on the door handle, he quickly pulled me away and said, "You have to kiss me before you go in. Now we can have sex. Seeing that we are going to be married, that child needs some mannish water to grow strong."

"What would God say about that?"

"We can pray for forgiveness after."

He had a one track mind, and he obviously was not thinking about the people we just passed next door who were sitting on the bench enjoying the moonlight with a full view of everything around. I could even see my friend peeping behind the curtain. She did not even think of turning off the lights before she looked.

"Look around you," I said to him, "And see how many eyes are upon us; even the moon looks like it is laughing at you."

Foolishly enough, he looked up at the moon. That was my chance to run to the house. I closed the door behind me while bidding him goodnight and goodbye. He just continued standing at the door, and my friend appeared to be stuck by her bedroom window. Neither of them had guessed I was going to move so fast.

I went to my bedroom, then back to the washroom for a bath. Sleep came to me quickly. I did not even hear the dogs bark that night or know what I had dreamt of. The next morning I woke up feeling fine, no morning sickness and an insatiable appetite. I could hear the noise of pots and pans in the kitchen.

The two children were still sleeping. I always helped out with the children in the morning, getting them ready for school, which was a difficult task for their mother. I had found a way to charm them, so that they cooperated with me willingly. I would sing until the boy opened his eyes. Maybe he could not handle my singing, so to get me stop, he would jump out of bed. I promised the older one five pennies to buy candies on Friday. She just lived for those Fridays.

When I walked into the kitchen, eggs and toast were already prepared for breakfast. My friend pointed to a bowl, told me it was my lunch, and walked away. The thermos no longer contained enough food for two. From now on, I was given cold food. As I walked to work, the lid on the bowl kept slipping off because it did not fit properly. I waited until I was in an open field where some cows were grazing, and I took out the bowl and drank all of the liquid leaving the meat, dumplings, and yam. I was all alone because my so-called friend did not walk to work with me.

6
All Things Work Together for Good

One week rolled into another, and my friend still did not say much to me. I knew that since I was living in her home I should reach out to her. Sometimes she'd give a half smile or she would pretend not to hear me.

Many things happen in our lives, and we ask the Lord "Why?" The Bible says that in everything we should give thanks, but sometimes it is hard to look up when you are in pain. We often focus on the pain in our minds and try to fix the circumstances around us.

I always love the middle of the week because I could begin looking forward to the weekend. This Wednesday morning began like any other day. I woke and got ready for work. The day was hot, the sun was bright, and the boss' face looked grumpy.

Only two men worked with us on the floor as fabric cutters. We all got along with each other. I saw my so-called friend early that morning talking with the men. I thought nothing of it, seeing that we all have to talk with them at some point in the day. A little while before the bell rang signaling the end of the day, my friend called the two men over to her machine and said to them, "Don't forget what we talked about." They smiled and walked away.

Five minutes before the bell, she called out to them again saying, "I'm counting on you guys."

We were in our small groups walking home when she decided to take a shortcut. I continued walking my usual route; everyone in the group had gone to her own home. I was the only one left. I decided to stroll slowly home. Looking up the hill I could see the preacher's house with its shut door meaning no one was home.

Walking up to my friend's front door, a sharp pain struck me, and I felt like I had been kicked in the mouth by a donkey. I dropped my bag and crouched on my knees for about five minutes. Then, when I decided to straighten up, the next pain struck me. I hurried to the door, ran into my bedroom, and crawled under the covers. I began rolling in pain, biting the pillow. I then asked God why I was feeling all this pains when I was fine all day.

About ten minutes later I heard a knock at the front door. Still biting the pillow, I went to see who it was. To my surprise, standing in front of me were the two men from work.

"What are you doing here?"

"Jen invited us to come."

"She's not here and I do not know when she will be back because the children are not here either."

The older guy said, "She told us to wait until she returned."

My pain got worse, and I began to cry. Feeling sorry for me, the one said, "Tell her we will talk at work tomorrow."

I ran crying to my room. Never in my life had I ever felt so much pain at once. I'd never had a toothache before either.

About eight o'clock, Jen walked through the front door and called to me, "Your fiancé is here and would like to talk with you."

I thought she was joking. I should have known she was not on my side anymore. I did not move so one of her children came in and told me it was true. When I left my bedroom, the preacher stood in front of me with his flat wide nostrils flared, yelling, "Where are you hiding your men? You country *****!"

With my toothache still unbearable, I tried to explain, and then my brain began processing the scenario as it would have played out had it not been for my toothache. I turned to my so-called friend and told her that the two guys from work that she had invited over wanted to stay because she had asked them to. I informed her that I had told them that I did not know when she would be returning home. Her countenance fell when she realized that her plan had not worked. She had set up for the two men to come to our house while she went and called George. She told him that I was involved with two other men and she had to put up with it in her own home. She thought she would have the preacher catch me in some act with the two men. God alone knows what she told them to do to me.

I returned to my room, fell on my knees, and thanked the Lord for the toothache. If it had not been for the toothache, I would have asked the men to come in and wait for Jen, just to be polite. I never thought anyone could be so evil. The preacher and Jen sat in the living room talking long after I left; I never knew when he left for home because I fell asleep.

Early Thursday I went to the dentist to get my tooth removed. He asked me which tooth he should pull out. I could not say because the pain was no longer there, but I could remember where the pain was the previous night.

Pointing to one of my teeth, the dentist said, "That is looking fine, but maybe it's all inside." He began to pull, and I felt that my brain was about to explode. After pulling the tooth, he washed it off, looked at it, and said, "I cannot see any cavity. All your teeth are looking fine. Well, we cannot do anything for this one now."

On my way home the Lord spoke to me telling me He sent the pain to protect me from what Jen had in store for me. I began to look at my situation seriously. I was not safe around her anymore. When I got home, no one was there so I slept the day away.

In the evening I went to see the preacher to continue talking about what went on the day before. Still spitting from having my tooth pulled, I decided to walk with a spit pan since I was afraid to let people see me spitting. I walked up to his door and knocked.

His sister looked out and then shouted, "Someone is here to see you."

I started walking up the steps as his sister came and stood in the doorway. The preacher shouted to her, "Let whoever it is in." She rolled her eyes in disgust then walked away.

I entered the living room and found George sitting at his machine repairing a shirt. He got up immediately and said, "Let's go outside and talk. I know my sister wants to know my plans."

As soon as we were safely outside, I asked, "Could you explain what happened yesterday with Jen?"

"Well, she came here yesterday to inform me about you and two guys at work. She asked me to come over and see for myself and kept on asking me how I could get married to someone like you? I almost told her about the child you are carrying and how you want to pass it off on me. When she asked me to come and see for myself, I kept quiet. I was thinking of going up the country to tell your mother the wedding is off and that you are pregnant by some other guy. If Jen had not said to come and see for myself, I was going to take the first bus to Georgetown and tell you mother all about what your friend said. I never knew Jen to be like that; she was a good friend of my mother."

I thank God for Jesus; He's always been there for me. He fights battles that I am not even aware of. I then told George about the changes in my relationship with Jen since I told her about the wedding.

After some thought, George said, "I'll ask my older brother and his wife if you can stay with them until the wedding."

We sat on the stoop for a long time. The moon was overhead with no clouds in the sky, just the bright shining moon. Next to the house was a large plant with some branches hanging out that cast a shadow. Pointing to the shadowy dark spot, the preacher said, "Let's go over there. My sister can't see us."

Thinking quickly, I asked "What about your neighbor who you said always looks over the bushy hedge?"

"Oh yes, I forgot that."

"And you also forgot about God."

"I didn't forget, but after that day all I can think about is having sex with you. It's not like we are just going around. In God's eyes you are my wife."

Not knowing what else to say, I blurted out, "But I just had my tooth pulled out and I'm still in pain."

"It will take the pain away," he said leaning toward me. "The first time, everything was so sudden I did not enjoy it because you fought like a tiger."

As he reminded me of that day, my body began to shake. His hand started traveling under my skirt, and his other hand began touching my hair. Watching the sweat pour from his face, I couldn't understand why he was perspiring when the night was so cool. Just then, the nosey neighbor decided to peep through the bushes. The preacher shouted something about people keeping their eyes in their own yards, and the neighbor disappeared and slammed her door. Personally, I was glad that lady came out because it stopped George.

It was now midnight and the moon lit up the surrounding area like day only without the heat. People were out enjoying the moonlight. Some were sitting at the roadside; others were kissing. You could not walk far without seeing couples doing what most couples do. We walked in silence. He was angry about the neighbor coming outside and looking across at us. As we reached the door of my friend's house, he said, "Don't forget, we are almost married," and he pulled me close to him for a kiss. I showed him my spit pan, and he pushed me away.

Closing the door behind me, I walked slowly to my room and threw myself across the bed. I looked up at the ceiling and thought about keeping myself sexually pure and being adamant about it until the preacher and I finally got married.

Saturday morning, his youngest sister came to see me. She was the only one that spoke with me as a friend. She told me her father wanted to see me and he seemed upset. Still in my pajamas, I told her to wait for me.

Her father knew I got paid every Friday, but when he saw my empty hands, his face looked even angrier. I greeted him but did not get any response; instead he began to talk to me indirectly. I told him that I understood exactly what he was saying. He did not look me in the eyes.

Turning his back to me, he said, "All the young girls come to me when they are in trouble and don't want anyone to know. I can help you. I'll smoke the child out of you with hot water, and no one will know you are with child before the wedding."

What he did not know was George had already told me about his father having young pregnant girls come to him to destroy their babies. He would kill the baby and then tell the girl to come back for a follow-up. This man was not a doctor and could not even spell or write his name. When the girls went back for their "follow-up," he would impregnate them again. This man wanted to have his cake and eat it too. He wanted to destroy his own offspring for his own gain.

I stood there looking at this man talking and answering himself and I understood where George got his behavior from. His father did not want me to marry his son fearing George would stop giving him money. He was still talking with his back towards me so he did not know when I left. I went and told the preacher all that his father had told me.

"I know my father can remove the child since you are still in the early stage, but he will have to have sex with you before he can do it and after. I, however, will not share you with my father. The wedding will go on as planned. I told your father we are going to be married." Changing the subject, he added, "My brother said you can come tomorrow to stay for a while."

That was good news because I could move from my so-called friend's house who no longer spoke to me. I waited until it was dark to pack all my belongings, and then I thanked Jen for the time I stayed in her home and all that she had done for me. The children ran to me asking when I would return. I told them I would not be living there anymore, and they began to cry. Their mother shouted at them to shut up, but they cried even more. I kissed the children goodbye and closed the door behind me. I also closed the door of friendship and trust with Jen.

Since George's brother's house was just around the corner from his, the preacher was standing outside waiting to help me with my bags. We walked towards his brother's home with the preacher carrying the larger bag. Every time he saw a car coming in our direction, he put the bag down behind him until the car was gone.

"Why do you keep putting my bag on the ground?"

"I don't want anyone to see me with a bag because they might be someone I preached to."

"So what if people do see you carrying a big bag?"

"You don't understand. Country people are accustomed to carrying a load, but not a preacher." He continued to mumble on, and I felt tempted to answer, but I remembered that I was at his mercy on the street with my bags. I consciously maintained my silence.

At the time, staying at his brother's home sounded like a good idea, but almost immediately I felt trapped. Every night the preacher came to visit me, and he never left until the first cock crowed the next day. Each evening, he would talk with his brother and then call me out on the porch. He sat high on the wall and told me to sit low so no one could see me. The house was close to the road, and people would pass by and call out to him. Sometimes he would push my head down lower when an elder of the church was passing by because the elder knew George should be at home preparing for the Sunday morning service. His excuse for staying every night was "I need something to remember you, so when the girls come around, I'll see you in my mind."

On that first night, about one o'clock in the morning, the road quieted down, and George came down from the wall. He pulled me close to him and began what would become his customary speech. "You know you are almost my wife, and after we finish having sex, I will ask God to forgive us. The Bible says that the man is the head and, if you are going to be my wife, you must obey me. After all, I did choose you."

One night after giving me his customary speech, he said, "Let me teach you something new. I don't like to eat food one way." I asked him what he was talking about, and he proceeded to whisper in my ear the intimate details about what he meant. He then forced himself on me, and I begged for him to stop because I was feeling dizzy, but he shouted back to shut up because I would wake his brother and wife. I told him that I was in pain, and he replied that all the other girls loved it and that if I didn't give him what he wanted, he would not be happy.

All of a sudden a bright light went on across the road. Apparently, George never thought of the house opposite the road. He thought that once it was dark, all was well. He dropped me on my head placing his foot on me saying, "Stay down. Stay down." I knew the neighbor was looking at us. He began to blame me as he always did when anything went wrong. And then he told me I caused people to look at him because of my loud mouth; he walked off the porch.

Our wedding day was approaching, and his boss' wife told him she needed me to try on my dress. Before I went, George told me not to let her see my body because she was a nurse and could discern that I was pregnant. What he failed to notice was that each day my hips looked larger anyway.

I was upstairs above the tailor shop about to try on my wedding dress, when someone knocked on the door. The boss' wife went to see who it was, and I could hear George outside asking her to call me out because he had something to say to me. She told him that he wasn't allowed to see the dress until the wedding day. Since I was just about to unzip my skirt when I heard his voice and I hadn't changed yet, I went to see what he wanted.

He pulled me outside and whispered, "Don't forget what we talked about. Don't let her see you change." His back was towards the door so he did not see the boss' wife looking at us. She came closer and asked if everything was okay. His frown quickly changed to a smile, and he indicated that everything was fine.

I think the lady overheard his words to me because when we went back inside, she sat down on the bed and told me to try on my dress. When I tried to zip up the dress, I could only go halfway. The lady came over, placed her hands on my middle section, and said, "You put on weight. Look at your navel pointing."

I did not answer, so she smiled and walked away. I could see the hard line on her face. I'm sure she was thinking, "The man in the tailor shop, who preaches to us, gets a young girl pregnant."

The preacher was still waiting outside. As I stepped out, he asked, "So, how was it?"

"She knows because the dress would not fit because of my mid-section."

George hung his head and walked away. He walked me back to the bus in silence.

Later that night, he said to me, "I went and told my boss to tell his wife to keep her mouth shut and to not say a word to the guys in the shop. My boss said he will try to talk with her. Some men just don't know how to handle women. I knew he was disappointed in me seeing that I often tell them about God, but he says he understands because men have needs. I told him that it wasn't my fault, but that it was you that made me fall." Once again he justified his actions by saying I had nothing to lose, but he had a reputation to keep.

I went inside and locked my bedroom door. Placing the pillow over my head I fell asleep.

Wednesday evening was prayer meeting and, since it was dark outside and the walk to church long, I went to George's house to wait for him. His sister was making supper while he was seated at the table putting scriptures together for his sermon. He did not wait for his supper when he saw me. On our way out he said, "Don't feel uncomfortable because I am being quiet. I'm meditating on my sermon." I secretly cherished the silence as we walked.

When we arrived at the church, the door was shut and locked. I walked to the house of the lady who was responsible for opening the church building. She was running late and was glad to see me. She gave me the keys, and I returned to find the preacher shaking one leg, a habit he had when he was concentrating. I shook the keys to let him know I was back.

We turned the lights on, and people began to enter one by one. I sat at the very back, and George took his seat in the front row. The song leader started the service, and after four songs the preacher went to the pulpit.

"Good night, everyone. It's nice to see so many people out. Many of us do not like prayer meetings, but the Lord wants us to pray always. My topic tonight is holiness. God wants us to be holy because he is a holy God. What is holiness? Holiness is to live a clean life before God each day; always going to Him to confess our sins." He continued on about living holy, and at the end he closed his Bible and said, "Let us be holy by going to God and confessing our sins."

After a big "amen," the people separated and knelt in groups. The men had their own group, and their voices were loud enough to drown out the voices of the ladies. I was alone observing their prayer time. I noticed that the preacher lifted himself up and down beating the bench as he prayed, "My Lord, help us to do right because you need a holy people."

The group of ladies in front of me began to gossip about all that was happening in other people's lives. A lady butted in saying, "Oh, I heard that last week. That is stale news as she is back at home with her mother."

I did not pray nor did I pretend to be praying. I looked across at the group of men and wondered about their personal lives. Around nine o'clock, a brother began to sing, which was the clue for the others to stop praying. We all got up and sat on the benches as a brother closed in prayer.

After church I started shaking hands with the others. Suddenly, my fiancé was standing next to me. As the church sisters came up to me, he would cut them off from talking to me.

We all left the church heading to our homes. The only light on the street was next to the police station, and the moon wasn't up yet. The remainder of our walk was dark, and George told me not to walk so fast and let the others pass by. I knew that he was up to no good. As we reached a corner with big trees and bushes, he said, "Stop, this is a good place to go behind that big tree."

Holding my hand, he led me through some bushes and stopped under a big tree. When he had his satisfaction, he ran out leaving me there groping for my underwear and Bible in the darkness. Standing at the edge of the road, George called out, "Hurry up, you fool, someone is coming!"

I did not have time to put my underwear on, so I stuffed it into my top. I was in total disgust all the way home, especially as he spoke about how he was doing this for the baby. "That is strength for you and the child, don't you know that?"

"If this is for the child," I asked, "Then how come you are the only one who is enjoying it?"

He changed the subject and began telling me how I needed to wear shoes with higher heels because I reminded him of a girlfriend he had. "She was so small," he jokingly said, "I could have put her in my back pocket." He laughed as he went on about how her head only reached his waist. Then he continued, "I have to see what kind of shoe you are going to buy for the wedding, I'm not going to bend down to kiss you when the minister says 'You may kiss the bride.'"

My father had already given a hundred dollars to buy my shoes. The money was in George's hand, and we had already made plans for us to go shoe shopping on Saturday. That day, we walked from store to store, and he detested all of my choices. All the shoes were too flat for him. We were at the last store, and the lady showed him a very high shoe and asked me to try it on. The shoe fit, but I could not walk in it because the heels were as thin as a pencil. (I don't mind a high shoe if the heels are thick.)

"I'll take this one," he said to the store clerk. We left with the shoes that made me dance even if I didn't want to. George told me, "All you have to do is put on the shoes and walk a bit every day until the wedding."

We met a lot of people in town that day that asked the same question, "Are you ready for the big day?" Each time they asked my heart would skip a beat. The word marriage sounded like a death sentence waiting for me. Each day that I spent with the preacher made me feel as though a small part of me was being taken away.

7
Death of an Innocent Lamb

In the Garden of Eden, when the first man and woman sinned, God killed an innocent lamb to cover their nakedness. That lamb was also a symbol of Christ's death for the world. The skin from the lamb was made to cover Adam and Eve's nakedness.

The day before the wedding, I went home. Everyone was involved with the preparations. My grandmother gave my father a large rooster for the wedding. My father tied it in the yard, along with a sheep he had bought. I was told that the person whom my father bought the sheep from said it had never been with young. Walking up to the sheep, I placed my hand on its head and a feeling of guilt came over me. Talking to the sheep, I told it that it was because of me that it was going to die. I felt something special towards the sheep but I just could not grasp what it was. It began to lick my hand, but my mom called out, "Don't get too attached to the sheep, the guy will be here soon to kill it. Come and let me style your hair." She took a hot comb and placed it on the burner and began to curl my hair.

A man walked into the yard with two large knives with very sharp edges. All the neighborhood children came over to see the sheep killed. The man led the sheep behind the kitchen. The children walked slowly behind him. I then told my mom I wanted to be there for the sheep. She refused and added, "No, you will just make it harder for the process to take place." About ten minutes later, one of my brothers came running towards us saying the sheep has a young one in its belly. My heart skipped a beat, and then I remembered the feelings I had towards the sheep and connected my feelings with the news I had just received. My mind went back to the Garden of Eden where a lamb died to cover man's sin, so this innocent lamb was to cover up my pregnancy. Everyone thought the sheep was just fat, but I felt something was not right.

Saturday morning felt like dooms day; it was my last day of being a single person. I had just turned seventeen the previous month, and I was already a mother and soon to be a wife. This was one cup of tea I found too hot to drink; yes, the cup of responsibility that came on all at once. I looked at myself as a little less than a person about to be given a ring of ownership just as animals were branded. I would be making a pledge to a minister for better or for worst. All I could see was that maybe it would be better if I tried to be a good wife as he said.

My bags were all packed, and everyone was busy preparing things for the wedding. No one seemed to notice that I was sad. The day reminded me of Christmas – everyone is busy for the big day, but they forget who the day is for. Not even my mother came and spoke to me or even said goodbye. I called to my mother, who was in the kitchen getting the drinks ready to send to the reception hall. I hollered, "I'm going now, mom," and she shouted "Okay," and that was it.

Walking out of the yard with a big lump in my throat, I could hear my younger siblings playing in the yard. They did not see when I walked out. It seemed to me that I was quickly ushered, though it may not have been intentional, away from my family. If I could have cried, I would have, but because of all the pains in my life through the years, it seemed that my fountain had dried up. A numb feeling was over me for the entire day. I knew what needed to be done, so I did it without any emotions.

I went to the fashion designer's home to dress and waited until it was time to go to the church. I did not even have a rose to hold in my hand. The preacher controlled the money and did not see the need for me to have roses. A sister, who came to help me dress, gave me some yellow flowers from her garden. She told me, "At the last moment I just felt to pick some flowers from my garden and bring them along." If she did not bring those flowers, I would have been the flowerless bride.

At one-thirty in the afternoon, I entered the washroom, locked the door, and just sat on the floor staring at the dots on the wall. The wedding was at three o'clock. I was interrupted by a sharp knock on the door and someone saying it was two o'clock and she needed to use the washroom too. I quickly turned on the shower, jumped under the water, and back out.

The room was filled with girls, some shining their shoes, other taking out rollers from their hair. There was lots of talking and laughing; everyone was telling me to smile, but I just couldn't. When I picked up my dress, it began to bounce in my hand. The cloth was a heavy spandex material. To me, the dress looked like something to sleep in. I found it to be despicable. The train of the dress was very long too. Someone had once told me not to have a long train, because the longer the train the longer the marital trouble you will have. I realized it was an old wives tale and a lie.

Then we heard a car honking; everyone rushed to the window to see while I just sat there. All the cars were waiting for us, but I didn't know which car was for me. George had only told me that someone would come for me. All the girls scrambled around for their shoes and handbags and ran out of the room leaving me alone while I waited for help with my head piece. The cars began to pull out one after the other, and I could hear footsteps running up to the door; I thought it might be my helper, but it wasn't. All the cars drove off, and only a small white one was left. The car belonged to the lady who had made the despicable thing she called a wedding dress. She was shocked to see me and asked, "Where is every one?" She had just come back for the house keys and to lock my door. She began laughing and said, "Come, the car is waiting." They all seemed to forget that I was the one who was getting married, and the wedding couldn't start without the bride.

On my arrival at the church, everyone was standing outside. The church was hot inside because there was no fan to cool it down. My father and some of the people from the country were sitting in a pickup with the hood covered. When they saw me, everyone went inside. My father and I stood at the church door waiting for the organ to begin. I had never seen my dad looking so tired. Then my sister came to me and whispered,

"Dad is drunk, he made a rum punch and kept tasting it, and you know he never drinks."

The young ladies in the bridal party wore bright green dresses with black bands tied around their waists. One of the bridesmaids had decided to wear light green, a totally different color. The grooms all wore similar brown suits with a dark brown trim around their jackets. They were looking far better than the ladies. I could not be bothered with how everyone looked; I just wanted the nightmare to be over. If I had wings, I would have flown away for sure.

The organ began, and my dad took my hand as the guys and ladies formed a long double line with a lady at the side of each guy. Then my dad and I walked down the aisle. As we started walking, my feet began to wobble, swaying from side to side as my dad tried to keep us both steady. I do not know how I managed to move forward. As I walked down the aisle, I saw my friend who is George's cousin standing up front in case she wanted to whisper to me. My bouquet of yellow flowers was shaking because of my fright. I did not know what was going on. I felt totally disconnected from the entire event.

When the minister asked the question, "Who gives this woman to this man?" and my father replied, "I do," I felt all alone standing there. I looked at the monster face to face, and then looked back at my dad who was trying to keep his eyes open. If he was not so drunk, he would have seen the message that I was sending with my eyes. I stood there, and as the minister spoke, I felt more and more as though I needed to sit. Beads of sweat could be seen on everyone present. I began to feel both dizzy and hungry. When the next question was asked, for me to say "I do," there was a silence and then the minister asked again. George squeezed my finger to get me to respond. Instead of saying "I do," I said "yes." When I was asked for my left hand, I put out my right. My balance shifted from one side to the next because of my high heel shoes.

After the ceremony, we were all outside taking pictures when my lawful monster whispered, "You have all your family and people from the country, but I only have my brother with me and people who I do not know." With the same breath he said, "My guys are looking better than your ladies," which was true, but I did not care.

It is a long ride to the country for the reception, and George began to talk nonstop. When he saw that I was sleeping, he talked to the driver. I was awakened by the sound of the car horns signaling to the whole village that the wedding party had arrived. George's body was halfway out of the window waving to people whom he did not know. He just wanted to be remembered. Even thought it was late, he insisted the driver to go to the next village and honk the car horn. The driver did as requested.

When we arrived at the reception hall, it was overcrowded. It seemed as though the entire village was present. There was a mountain of gifts and people handed me envelopes. I thought they were just cards, and when my hands got full, I placed them on a bale and moved on. I never knew the envelopes contained money.

My mom came up for her speech and said, "Well, you all have taken a big step, but I hope when you have any problems, you don't come running back home to me like your father who never fully left his mother's home. It would be better that you stay and work it out on your own." My heart sank within me as a lump rose in my throat. I hung my head down with pain and shame, and I could see my monster husband smiling. It felt like my mother just openly signed my death warrant. I also felt uncomfortable that she used this occasion to embarrass my dad publicly. He was drunk and did not care about what she was saying. What a lot of women fail to understand is timing and where and how to get the point across.

Next to speak was my father, who looked more sober by this point. He began with the words, "Marriage is a good thing. It is like a plant and you have to take care of it. Take time to water it." Then he stopped and finally continued, "Nothing that starts wrong could end up right; I hope it comes out better than my marriage. Take care of each other." Everyone applauded him for his confession. Those words are words I'll never forget as long as I live. George turned and asked me if I told my dad anything about our relationship. I told him that I had not, but George didn't believe me, so I told him that my dad must have heard something about him. We were still seated at the bridal table so he kept his composure.

After my father finished his speech, everyone wanted to speak on my behalf. Some wore shoes while others were barefooted. The well dressed and those in their Sunday best came with gifts. There was plenty to eat and drink. Soon the time came for those who were living in town as well as the bride and groom to leave. I was just about to enter the car when an old man came up to me and handed me an envelope. He said, "I'm proud of you. I just wanted you to know." It was dark, so I drew a little closer to see his face. I could not believe my eyes; this was the second time that day that I was looking into the face of a monster. This man took me up to the pulpit and molested me at the age of nine. Thank God he could not stand on his third leg. He looked disappointed and ashamed because I was aware of his infidelity. He walked away quickly into the dark.

"Who was that man?" asked my husband who was also getting in the car.

"Nobody I care to know or wish to talk to."

George took the envelope given to me by the second monster and asked, "What is this?"

My mom came over with things for us to eat. She said, "Here is some meat and food so you will not have to cook tomorrow." She gave us a kiss and off we went, leaving my sister amazed that she could not stuff all the gifts into the car.

We had over a thousand gifts in our living room with some left at my mom's house. Later on that night, I was about to change when I noticed an envelope. I opened it to find a twenty dollar bill. I then remembered all the others placed on the table at the reception and that we had forgotten to go back for them. I knew that if I said anything to the preacher, I would not hear the end of it. He was in the living room opening gifts, so I joined him.

After a while he said, "Let's go to sleep, we have church in the morning."

"Church? They are not looking for us; they know we need time for our honeymoon."

"What honeymoon: all the honey already ran out of the moon. I can get it when I want, so what."

We lay on the bed and he talked about how good the day had gone and how everyone was able to eat and drink. Then we heard a knock on the front door. Wondering who could be visiting at one o'clock in the morning, George crawled out of bed. I could hear his brother's voice along with a friend asking for more food. George told his brother to take what he wanted and left the two to eat while he came back to the bedroom. All I could hear was laughing outside.

Turning to the preacher, I said, "I hope you did not give them all the food my mom gave us." Then the door slammed and they were gone.

George went to see what they did and came back inside complaining, "I can't believe that boy ate all the food. The big bowl of meat and everything else is gone."

"That is our Sunday meal!" I exclaimed. "You know your brother only thinks of himself. You should have given him some of it, instead of letting him eat whatever he wanted."

I did not get any answer and then I heard him snoring. I watched his large lips vibrate as he turned and placed his long legs across me. I did not want to push him, so I pretended to be rolling onto my side. I covered my head with the pillow and drifted off to sleep.

The next morning, I was awakened by someone touching my side. I could see the daylight coming through the window. I turned and looked at George who smiled and said, "Girl, you can snore." I asked him if that was all I did and he said yes. Then I said to him, "You did snore and more!" which he promptly denied.

He changed the subject to church. "I'm going to prove them wrong today; a man does not have to stay at home just because he got married. Let them see that God comes first for me." He did not have to preach that day because he had the week off. The elders had told him that he would need time for his new family but I guess he wanted to prove it to himself and them that he was "so spiritual."

"We don't have any food, just wedding cake. And I don't want to listen to you talk about being godly."

"I'll go and get some rice and chicken for us." He went to the shop at seven-thirty and returned home angry, throwing the food on the table. "When I ordered a pound of chicken, someone began to laugh. I turned to where the laughter was coming from and I saw my father with some other guys playing cards. One of them said to him, 'Is this your boy you was just talking about?' My father looked up at me and said, 'He is not my son.'"

His father was very angry with him because George had stood by his sister when their father wanted to put her out onto the street. His father told him not to take her in but to let her remain homeless at the age of fourteen. That was the first reason; the second reason for his anger was he was no longer receiving the amount of money he was used to from his son.

We did not have a fridge, so I cleaned the chicken, half filled the sink with water, and placed the bowl of chicken in the water to keep it fresh. Church was starting soon, and I noticed George was not getting ready. The walk to church took an hour, so I asked, "Are you still going to church?"

"Yes, but I want to get there when everyone is inside. I'm going to wear the suit that I got married in for those who did not see me yesterday."

When we arrived at church, he went up to the front and I sat at the back. After church, people began to ask if the church had a men's choir there because there were three other guys from the wedding that had arrived all dressed alike. Others were curious and wanted to know why George was at church. A loud mouthed guy came up to him and said, "My brother, I'm so happy for you, but don't you think God understands that you just got married and need time for your new family? I wish I had gotten married. They would not see me here for a month." Everyone began to laugh, and the brother walked away saying, "You are a joker my brother, a big joker." I could see that George was feeling ashamed. I wanted to laugh as well, but I controlled myself.

Back home I looked around to see what was left in the kitchen. His sister had taken almost everything. The preacher opened wedding gifts. After dinner I went behind the house and sat under a fruit tree where it was cool. I could hear sad love songs coming from the neighbor's house across the street from us. I called my preaching husband and asked who was playing the music because the person sounded like they were in pain. He called me inside and told me to sit, pointing to the chair.

"Let me tell you the story of my love life. The house that the music is coming from is my girlfriend's home. A lady whom I love with all my heart. She was to be my wife. We had a great sex life, and we often talked about our wedding. If she did not have a child already, I would have married her, but, as I told her, I wanted to be the first man to open the womb of the woman I marry. You see, she had a child when she was very young, and the child's father is living next door. She has told me that nothing is going on between them, and he only comes to see the child. The songs she is playing I can remember from every time we had a falling out; she would play them until I came knocking on her mother's door. I can feel her pain and I know what she is going through. I broke a promise that I made to her. I wish that I could hold her in my arms and tell her that everything will be okay."

I sat there looking at him with anger raging within me. I felt my heart freezing to cover the pain, and it stayed frozen. He went to the washroom to wash away the tears from his eyes. He turned the faucet on so as to minimize his distressed cries. I heard him open the window in the bathroom, so I tiptoed around the back of the house and saw him looking up the hill crying. The music played on into the night. I do not know if he came into bed at all.

The next morning he could not look me in the face. We both went to our places of work. My co-workers told me that my wedding had been a nice country wedding. At lunch time they told me, "Well, girl, you are married to a very good preacher man!" I just smiled as they all called me by my new last name. The ladies wanted to know how the honeymoon was and I told them that it was just as all honeymoons were – honey was just dripping from the moon. If anyone happened to walk under the moon at that time, they would be next to get married. They laughed and asked, "Does the moon have to be full or a new moon?" We all had a good laugh as we ate. They did not know that I was living in an ice box; things had gotten colder and colder between George and me. He would not talk to me except at church or around people as a cover up for what was really going on.

I was now seven months pregnant, and the heat in the garment factory made me sick. One day I fainted while sewing at the machine. My boss told me to stay home until the baby was born. I went home at midday, and, not long after I arrived home, I heard footsteps coming towards the front door.

"What are you doing home?" George demanded with his nostrils flaring. I asked him the same question, and he launched out and grabbed me while pushing me up against the wall. I told him why I had come home early and he got even angrier. Grabbing my feet he began to shake me, shouting, "I'm going to make this child come out of your mouth today." As he shook me up and down, I put out my hands to brace the fall. He then dropped me on my head and said, "The guy came asking for the money I borrowed to buy your wedding ring. The boss' wife wants her money also because I did not pay her last month. She told the guys that I got you pregnant before the wedding, and now I'm the laughing stock of the tailor shop. I got into an argument with the boss' wife and I told the boss that I'm not coming back there as long as she is there. When I got to work this morning everyone was silent with smirks on their faces. I don't know how some men can't keep their wives under control. Now you want to be rude to me?"

Because of my position on the floor, I really could not say anything because my tongue was swollen and was blocking my airway as I hung upside down. He went to the bedroom and grabbed his fishing pole and left the house. I wished that I had someone to talk to. I couldn't tell my mom; she had already warned me to not come running back to her with my problems and I did not have any friends in the area with whom I could talk to. Jesus was my only friend; I wrote letters to Him telling Him what happened before the wedding and up to the day my boss told me to stay at home until the baby was born. At the end of each letter, I would ask Him what He thought I should do. To post my letters, I flushed them down the toilet.

My preaching husband did not go back to his place of work. He decided to be self-employed and expected people to come and have clothing sewn. This became a time of financial hardship, and sometimes we had no food for several days.

One afternoon a car stopped in front of our gate. I could see the person; he was leaning over and slowly taking something from the car. I called to the preacher to come take a look. As he peeped through the door he shouted at me, "You fool, it's the boss!" I didn't know how that made me the fool; I did not know his boss had a new car. His boss entered our home with a big brown bag in front of him. My husband ordered me into the bedroom so that they could talk.

His boss apologized by saying, "I'm sorry things turned out the way they did. After you left, I had a talk with my wife but I know the damage is done. I would like you to come back. You are one of my best workers. I can put anything into your hands and it is done."

"How can I, with everyone laughing at me?" George's voice rose above his boss. "Your wife has destroyed my good name. No, boss, I will not come back, even if you pay me more, I will not set my foot in there."

The boss told him that he understood and asked if George could do the work from home. They settled on George working from home. So I wouldn't appear interested in their conversation, I closed the bedroom door and did not hear the rest of what was said.

When the boss left, I went to see what was in the bag. It was food.

"Why should I pay for something you don't even wear?" He was talking about the wedding dress and the ring. I knew that George still did not have any intention of paying the boss' wife. He was the one that handled all of the money that came through the home, and I had no say.

Things got a little better after that because the boss had work for George, and he would go fishing every night. We did not have a fridge, and most of the time we had no oil to fry the fish, so we had fish tea, fish for lunch and fish for dinner. When things were slow at the tailor shop, the boss gave the guys in the shop priority with the work.

One afternoon a co-worker of the preacher came to our home and told George how much he missed him. He told George that he should not let the boss' wife intimidate him. Just before leaving, the co-worker mentioned that the boss was sick and that he had had a stroke.

Three weeks went by before George finally went to see his boss, but the boss had suffered another stroke that affected his brain. When George tried to explain to his boss who he was, all the boss did was touch the clothing he was wearing. Saliva freely ran from the boss' mouth. His wife came and turned him to face the cartoons that were on the television.

George did not want his boss' wife to see him praying, so he told me to stand guard at the door. He began praying casting out spirits, telling them to leave this man because he was good man and to free his mind from the evil spirits. After praying for his boss, George began to curse the man's wife calling her a wicked witch. He blamed her for causing him to be in the position he was in. As George looked at me for support, I shook my head in agreement. I knew if I did not respond as though I agreed with him, he would become angry with me. The boss never got better, and he died.

I can remember another day when we went to visit a couple. They talked and laughed together, and then the man asked my preaching husband how his married life was going. George became so upset, began to curse the man, and wanted to fight him in his own home. He blamed everyone but himself for his life.

84

My heart goes out to some of the young men who came to George for advice and who then became rebellious in their own homes and churches. Some of them stopped going to church.

———◆◆☀◆◆———

I was now close to giving birth. George had stopped going fishing, and there was nothing in the house to eat. I went to the back of the house, sat under a tree, and leaned back with my hands in the dirt. I grabbed handfuls of dirt and stuffed them into my mouth. After eating the dirt, I drank some water. Dirt and water was my food for the day. The preacher was inside, still sleeping at eleven o'clock in the morning. We did not have any communication between us, so I went back outside to sit leaving him in the hot house. I thank God for the day when He said, "let the water under the heaven be gathered together and let dry land appear." (Genesis 1:9). I must say that the dry land and water came in handy that day when the little one began to kick within me for food.

Things were hard at home growing up, but I felt like I went from the pot into the fire. One Friday morning, I awoke to a warm feeling on my face. I opened my eyes to see the sun beaming through the window. I felt like staying in bed, but under my abdomen I began to feel stiff. I went to the washroom and then crawled back under the sheets. The preacher opened his eyes, looked at me, and then turned his back towards me. A cramping feeling began to come from my back to my side. I did not eat or drink all that day as the pain came and went. The pillow was my comfort as the pain became more unbearable than my hunger. The pain did not stop.

Saturday morning, I went to use the washroom and passed some thick water. I told George who became angry with me.

"You can't have the child now! What will people say about me? They will check the date of the wedding. It has to be later; this can't be happening to me." He began walking around inside the house with his hands on his head while I was in pain. All he could think of was himself. He turned back to me and said, "You better hold that in because you have to go to church tomorrow so they can see you are still pregnant."

I could not make the pain go away. George went into the washroom and returned with his hands full of things to rub. He told me to "take off everything and let me rub you down" so I did. He rubbed me from my neck to my toes, but the pain got worse. He emptied all of the contents on me and then took a blanket and covered me. He pointed his finger and admonished, "You stay there. I'm going out. You sweat out that cold."

The day was very hot, and I felt like I was going to pass out, but the pain always brought me back. My husband had refused to open any windows because he said the heat would help. My blankets were wet with sweat.

George never returned until nightfall. When he came in, he said, "I did not find anything to eat. I thought I'd find someone who had money for me. Is the pain gone?"

"No, it is even worse!"

We heard a knock at the front door, and he slammed the bedroom door behind him as he went to see who it was. I could hear the voice of his older brother. George came back to the bedroom and told me not to make a sound because he did not want his brother to know what was happening with me. They sat in the living room laughing and talking. As the pain got worse, I could not bite the pillow any longer. George rushed in and told me to be quiet because he could hear me crying outside.

After his brother left, George came in and told me his brother wanted money and borrowed it even though he already owed him. My pain was becoming more intense, so he took his pillow and said, "I'll be sleeping on the couch because it is impossible to sleep with you crying next to me."

About one o'clock Sunday morning, I began to bleed. My abdomen had dropped. Waddling out of the bedroom, I went to where George was snoring loudly on the couch. I touched him and startled him. He asked what I wanted and complained that he found it impossible to sleep.

"I don't have a cold. I'm bleeding. It must be the baby."

George knelt on the floor and began praying, "Lord, can you stop this for me? People are looking up to me."

"Stop praying and go find someone with a car," I hollered at him. "I need to go to the hospital."

I held up my belly as the waves of pain came. It felt as though everything was falling down to my feet.

George returned ten minutes later with a car. I climbed into the back, and he sat in the front with the driver. On our way, the driver kept looking back at me while the preacher held his head straight and conversed with the driver. At one point, the driver looked back and said, "We are almost there." No cars were on the road, so he was able to drive faster. I felt like all my strength was gone. Sleep wanted to overtake me, but nature kept telling me, "You have work to do."

When the car stopped in front of the hospital, a nurse came out and helped me onto my feet. She looked at me and then told me to sit as she ran hastily back inside the hospital shouting "Doctor! Doctor!" I was immediately surrounded by doctors and nurses. A doctor told them to take me up to the operating theatre.

In the operating theatre, the doctor examined me and told me that the baby should have been out already, but because I had such small hips, it couldn't come. The baby's heartbeat was very weak, and I did not have the strength. Before I could say a word, a nurse placed a breathing mask over my nose. I could hear the noise of knives and other equipment before I fell into a heavily sedated sleep.

When I awoke, a nurse was standing next to the bed. She smiled and said, "You are very lucky! You have a baby girl weighing ten pounds." She wanted to know what I ate during the pregnancy and I told her that I had eaten fish and green banana. Still sleepy, I closed my eyes and was awakened by another nurse who came to give me some medication. I did not see my baby or the preacher that day.

Early the next morning, a nurse came to help me tidy up. She told me that I had to try to feed the baby. They had given her some food, but she still wanted more. She told me that after I tidied myself up that I could see my baby. I asked the nurse if I could have something to eat, and she told me that I was not allowed food for three days but I could have a block of ice.

While talking with the nurse, I saw the preacher walking up to me holding a bundle in his hands. His face was looking at what he was holding, and he almost bumped into the nurse. As he came close, he held up his hand and with a big grin on his face asked, "You want to see my beautiful daughter?" He drew the bundle close to my face.

Seeing my baby girl was the most wonderful feeling I ever had. All my hunger left. Lying in that pink blanket was a baby who looked as though she was two months old. She was very pink with a full head of soft black curls and a big round face. I pulled the blanket back to count the toes and fingers. I was in shock at what I saw! I counted ten toes then went to the fingers and counted eleven. There was a little finger with a nail just hanging at the side of one hand. I could remember that my mom said that one of my brothers was born with eleven fingers, but we did not see it because she had it cut off.

George commented on how big she was. He said that it was because of all the fish we ate and how now he could see how mucho of a man he was. Walking back to the nursery, he danced with the baby in his arms. Five minutes before visiting hours were up, he came to my bedside and whispered, "Now you can't let anyone know you are in here. I'll try to get you home without anyone knowing. When I'm ready, I'll tell them."

I outwardly agreed with him, but in my mind I wondered how I would be able to tell anyone when I couldn't walk and didn't know anyone around me.

Just as George finished talking, a lady called out to him and said, "I didn't know your wife had the baby already!"

George hung his head down and said, "Oh yes, she had a fall trying to put some clothes on the line."

When the lady walked away, he turned to me and warned, "You better stick to the story. I'm going to write your mother a letter and tell her the same thing. I will give the letter to one of the country bus drivers to take to her." He then walked away.

The next day he arrived very early to visit his daughter. I could hear his voice; he spent all his time in the nursery with her until visiting hours were up.

Finally, after seven days, a nurse said to me, "You will be going home today."

I was packing my things when the preacher came to see his daughter as he always did. The nurse told him that I was discharged from the hospital that morning. He came with the baby and asked, "Are you ready?"

I climbed slowly from the bed, took my bag, and walked behind him and the baby. We stood at the side of the road waiting for a van to take us home. The first one was too full, and it only had room for one. Standing there feeling weak, I began to pray that a van would come soon, and one did with room for two. My husband climbed in first leaving me standing there. The conductor saw I could not climb in on my own, so he came and gently helped me into the van. George sat there smiling from ear to ear while holding the baby.

It felt good to be home and away from the busy hospital. I went into the bedroom to change, and the baby was on our bed. I heard the sound of a spoon removing food from a pot. George pushed his head into the bedroom and said, "I have some food here if you want some. Say now before all is gone."

"No thanks," I told him because I sensed that he did not really want to share. I heard the spoon moving around the inside of the pot for some time while I rested on the bed with the baby. About twenty minutes later, George came into the bedroom wearing only a condom. As he stood over me, I looked at him and asked him what was going on.

"God said the only time I can stay away from sex is for prayer and fasting. I waited seven days; now it's time." Uncovering my lower body, he made his way into the bed.

"What about my stitches? I'm still sore."

"Since you did not deliver the child on your own, you are fine. I'm not touching your abdomen. Just be quiet." Leaning over, he then whispered in my ear, "You think I don't care about you. Why do you think I'm wearing a condom?"

I lay there like I was dead as he rocked my body up and down and from side to side. I asked God if this was all a woman was to be – a slave to people like this.

After George was through, he commented, "That was not so bad after all." I did not answer him, so he looked at my face and repeated what he had said. Before I could respond, he was on his back asleep and snoring.

That night, we were awakened by the cry of the baby. He got up, gave her a bottle, and then changed her. I never heard him thank God that I had not gone along with him and his father to kill the child in me.

The baby ate like a small horse, and my husband still was not making enough money to buy food. Sometimes he would only catch a few fish, and I did not have any breast milk because of lack of food. On Sundays he would invite himself to the homes of people in the church in order to have a Sunday meal. Going to the homes of these people made me feel like an outcast. The comments often made by the ladies of the homes were a strong indication that they had wanted their daughters to marry the preacher.

One lady told George how the child did not take after me. She went on to say that her family's blood was very strong. She felt that if he had married her daughter, Judie, there would have been a resemblance in the child. Placing the food in front of him, the mother went on to say that the dish was made by Judie. George sat there like a king complimenting Judie's dish with words I'd never heard him utter to me. As we ate, the young girl took my baby and walked around with her as her mother continued talking about how good her daughter was in the kitchen. Judie was standing in front of a large mirror with the baby's face close to hers. She did not know that I was watching every move she made with my child. Maybe she was wondering about what her mother said – if she and the preacher had had a child that the child would have shared a resemblance.

8
Ask and It shall be Given

The next Sunday night, my husband was preaching, and I stayed home with the baby. Those were my best moments alone with God, walking from the bedroom to the living room talking. I went and opened the cupboard. Yes, the Lord had provided food for that day, but what about the coming days? I began to call on Him saying, "Come, God, come take a look. No milk, no sugar, no salt, just empty tin cans. I can't bear it. What about the child? Is this a punishment for me? I preserved this child's life because I believed that you wanted her to survive. Lord, if I did the right thing, then send food for her. My husband does not want me to go back and work. He told me that he is the man of his house." As I ended my talk with God, I began thanking him for sugar, milk, rice, meat, and everything that I could think of. I gave him a list of things and then I went to bed.

On Monday morning, the baby was the first one up. She began crying, and I threw the covers off and rushed to her. When she cried, she expected you to be there. It seemed as though her notes and the pitch could break glass. I took her up and went to the kitchen. There was an orange on the kitchen table. Still rocking the baby, I stood at the window looking over at my neighbor's garden with all kinds of food to eat. I consciously withdrew my mind from lusting after what was not mine. I picked up the orange and rolled it on the floor before cutting it so as to get more juice from it. I squeezed the orange in anger. All I got was two ounces. Two pulls on the nipple, and my daughter was pulling on air. I decided to open the window, and as I pushed the top window, I saw a car pull up. It was a man from the church. After getting out of his car, the heavy set man struggled to climb the stairs while carrying a bag.

Halfway up the stairs, the man began to call out. He saw me and said, "Call your husband." But I could not move, until he called my name. I went and got the preacher who was still sleeping. The two shook hands, then holding the bag on each side, they entered the house. The man was still trying to catch his breath, but spoke, "Well, my friend, sorry to wake you, but this was the only time I could make it. As you know my work is to deliver goods to different stores and when there are any damaged goods, they give it to us, so I brought some things for you all. Also, I would like you to make me some clothes. Here is a down payment of three hundred dollars."

I stood there with my heart beating in excitement as I quietly prayed, "Lord, you did it, you did it!" I could not contain myself, so I went to the bedroom and began to laugh for joy. I knew the men outside were thinking that I was laughing with my daughter. After the man left, I hurried out of the bedroom to see what was in the big bag. To my surprise, all I could say was "He did it!" I found rice, flour, sugar, and milk for us and the baby! I even got things that I was not able to buy in the supermarket. We had food to last for a month. The Lord showed me that my decision to save my baby's life was the right thing to do.

My daughter continued to grow strong. Her father called her "daddy's girl."

9

How Green is the Grass

While we had food to eat, we still did not have enough money to pay the bills. I told George that seeing as he was working at home, I could go back to work while he looked after the baby. I thought it was a good idea. He got angry, slammed me up against the wall, and said, "What do you think people will say? That I can't take care of my family! You know what the Bible says about people who can't look after their own? They are worse than an infidel. So you see how you always want to undermine my good name." The baby began to cry because of the anger and change in the atmosphere of the room. He went over to our daughter, picked her up, and crooned, "Don't cry, daddy's girl. That foolish woman wants to destroy me."

Later that same afternoon, a former coworker came to see the preacher. He told George how much they missed him in the tailor shop since the boss died and his wife took over. Then he mentioned that the guys were leaving.

"Where are they leaving to go?" George asked.

"To Trinidad. I hear that the grass is greener over there. We got a letter from one of the guys. He said the pay is very good. His boss pays him three times the amount we are getting now, and you know he was not a number one tailor. He also said he gave his boss your address and told him all about you. His boss will be coming over to St. Vincent at the end of this month to see you. He is planning to take you back with him, all expenses paid. You can live like a king with the money you will be making. So are you going? Just tell the boss when he comes to see you that I'm a good worker too."

The preacher's eyes lit up as he smiled from ear to ear. He sat back with his two hands behind his head. "You brought good news! Man, you think I'm going to let a good deal like that pass me by? I can even go and take over the shop. Who knows, I might even put the guy out of business and make a name for myself. This guy has the money, but I'm the tailor!"

I peeked discreetly through the bedroom door and could see them in the living room. His ex-coworker displayed a look of surprise at the answer George gave.

At the end of the month, the preacher got a visit from a big, tall, bald dark guy who looked like Mr. T. with gold chains around his neck and even a gold tooth. The men spoke outside of the house for a very long time. After the man left, George returned to the house in smiles. I knew not to ask what was said because if he wanted to talk he would. He immediately went to the closet, dressed, and left the house. I had a feeling that he went to see the pastor to tell him of his plans. I did not hear the conversation with him and the Mr. T. Lookalike, but I began to wonder as to whether George said yes to this man or not and if he would be leaving soon and whether he would take us along. I had more questions than answers in my mind.

George returned around midnight. I woke up to the sound of the front door being closed noisily. He entered the bedroom, threw himself on the bed, and began shouting, "I don't know why certain people that call themselves Christian talk about love, and when it comes time to show it, they speak contrary to love."

I pointed to the baby crib that was next to our bed, and he got the message and lowered his voice. We went to the living room where he began to tell me that he went to the pastor to let him know the good news of what God had done.

"What has God done?"

"You are like the rest of them who don't want to see me get ahead!" His voice rose again.

I did not answer him.

He then told me how Mr. T. Lookalike wanted him to leave for Trinidad. A room was already waiting for him and later on he would get a house so that we could all be there together as a family. The preacher continued, "He gave me the money for my airfare. I thought my beloved pastor would be happy for me but he disappointed me. He wants me to stay in St. Vincent and questioned if I asked God about it. What is there to ask about when God sent this man from miles away to get me? This is a chance of a lifetime and no one is going to stop me!"

A few days later on Sunday, we went to church and the pastor preached a message entitled "Is It God's Will?" He spoke about people who are walking out of God's will while refusing to ask God if it is His will. Not everything that seems good is always the will of God.

After church George did not stay around to chat as he always did. He left immediately and walked swiftly as I ran short steps to keep up with his pace. He was silent on the way home. As he entered the front door, he said to me, "I am going to buy myself a plane ticket for Trinidad tomorrow. You will have to go back and live with your mother. I have already asked someone to stay in our house. My older brother will collect the rent and put it in the bank for me. Some will go towards the mortgage."

On Friday my daughter and I stood at the airport waving goodbye to George. My mother came and helped me pack, and we all went back to the country. My mom fed my daughter and myself with whatever she could. I was feeling a sense of freedom, but still felt bound when I remembered the preacher. He sent money for us whenever he could.

One day I got a message from the airline stating that two tickets were waiting for my daughter and me. My daughter was now one year old and still was not walking properly. I went to pick up the tickets and was told that we only had one week to fly out of St. Vincent. My mom helped me put things together for the long trip. The day before leaving I made a promise to her that I would send for her. She looked at me and laughed. I told my daughter that she was going to meet her dad and she seemed to understand what I was saying.

On our arrival to Trinidad airport, the officer asked where we were going. My daughter began to shout excitedly, "Daddy! Daddy!" She was pointing to the officer. The officer asked me if her father was over where she was pointing, but I did not answer, pretending to calm my daughter down. He then stamped my passport.

George was waiting outside with some people from the church he attended. They came to help in case I had any problem getting through with immigration. When George saw us, he came running towards us. He took his daughter and threw her up into the air and shouted, "Daddy's girl is here!" He said to the crowd, "This is my wife." I never thought it fit that he didn't introduce me by name.

We then headed to our new home. The car pulled up in front of a large house. My eyes opened wide and I was eager to see the inside. As George opened the door, I pushed my way in first. The house was well furnished. The living room had a good big chair plus a large television, carpet on the floor, and beautiful bouquets of flowers at the corners and the center of the room. I went to see the bedroom. It had a large bed and carpet on the floor as well. The kitchen was not in the living room as it was in our old house but located next to the dining room. Everything I needed was in the kitchen – fridge, stove, and oven.

The preacher was in the living room getting reacquainted with his daughter asking her all kinds of questions, so I went to the bedroom to change. I was only in my half slip when I remembered to ask him a question. I rushed into the living room about to speak when George turned on the television. A man's face appeared and said, "Good evening." I dashed back into the bedroom feeling ashamed that this man had seen me half naked.

I called out to George and asked him why he did that.

"Did what?" he asked. So I told him that the man saw me half naked. "Come and let me show you something," laughed George. "The people can't see you, but you can see them."

He went on to show me how to turn the television on and off and how to switch to different stations. I was amazed that he did not call me a

96

fool. He told me that the house belonged to the boss whose wife was no longer living with him. The boss was letting us stay there as long as we wanted to rent free. George then told me the rules. "I don't want you outside. Always keep the doors locked. When I'm at work, don't answer the door, not even if it is my boss. I will show you what you need to know. The fridge is filled with food, and if you ever need anything, just call me at work and I can shop on my way home."

He took us twice to his place of work, and I made some mental landmarks of how to get there on my own. Two months later I took a taxi and went to his workplace. The boss was not there, so my husband was happy about that. He told me that the boss took away other men's wives or girlfriends for himself and that he didn't want me close to the boss. I explained to him that I had no intention of lowering my Christian values. He did not respond. There were some other guys working in the room as well. He wanted to know how I had gotten there and if the boss had anything to do with it. I told him that I had remembered the way. His comment was "So you know your way around."

About eight at night, a young lady walked in and asked who we were. George told her that we were his daughter and wife. She walked past me and sat at his machine, asking him how his day was so far. My daughter went close to look at the lady's face. Her back was turned, but I could see George's face. They talked and laughed as though I was not there. When she was about to leave, I realized that her tummy looked as though she was pregnant. George got up from his machine too and asked me to wait outside in the dark street with our daughter. They spent another twenty minutes inside alone, and then came out laughing. He walked her to the taxi stand and said goodnight to her. All this time I maintained my composure.

We hailed a taxi that was going our way, and as we entered the taxi, George started telling me how the woman was an old friend from St. Vincent and that they knew each other from childhood. "She was in love with me then, and still is. I know the guy she is living with, and he is a nobody. I told her that she can do better. Don't take her on; you see the way she is coming on to me? She is something else. She is carrying someone else's child but still in love with me."

As the taxi turned the corners, he leaned towards me, and his skin rubbed against mine. My body became like icicles, and his touch as a foreign object. The taxi driver kept looking back into his rearview mirror as the preacher kept talking. I did not say a word, just wondered what love felt like and what it was like to have someone who really loves you.

I whispered a silent word of prayer asking God to let me know what falling in love is like. I saw the tenderness George had shown the lady as he opened the car door and closed it telling her to have a good night. Imbedded in my heart was the cry for true love but I asked myself, "Will I know when it arrives?" My heart was blocked by huge mountains of ice, and my emotions were being destroyed.

I still wanted to know what romance was. I'm not talking about sex. God said your desire shall be for your husband. That word "desire" is what I'm talking about. (Genesis 4:16) Desire – to be loved or feel wanted. Was my experience part of the curse handed down to woman in the Garden of Eden? I knew that God loved me, but I often heard people say that they were in love or someone was in love with them. I knew the Bible said that a man should love his wife as Christ loves the church and gave himself for it. So, I wasn't asking for something impossible. Yes, I was looking for love, but I still felt afraid of uncovering something that could easily be destroyed.

Mothers, teach your sons to love. What is love if it has never been shown or taught? What is love if it never engulfs you? What is love if your heartbeat is only in your feet?

The taxi stopped in front of our house. Before we got out, the preacher asked what I had cooked for him. I pretended not to hear and continued to the door. As soon as we entered the house, I went to the kitchen and reheated some food for him. I stood in front of the fridge that was full of things to eat but did not have any appetite. I had a deep hole in my heart that food could not fill, a thirst that would not be quenched by water.

George was in the living room watching television, so I took his supper to him and then prepared something for my daughter to eat. We all sat there watching a movie. My eyes were looking at the television, but my mind was back at the tailor shop as questions began to run through my mind.

———————◆◈◆———————

One year rolled into another like demons of the night coming to visit the demons of the day. George now had lots of customers. Most were people from the church we attended, but he also took some of the boss' customers for himself. His regular work at the boss' tailor shop became too much for him to handle along with his personal work. Someone in the tailor shop told the boss what my husband was doing, and the boss became very angry with him. When the boss asked George why he was undermining him, he told the boss that he did not need him and that many people knew that he could sew without thinking of whose house he was living in and the fact that the boss knew that we were in Trinidad illegally.

I could have shown George what could happen to us when he said that he was going to tell the boss off for talking behind his back, but I decided to say nothing because my husband regarded me as a poor country girl without any brains as he reminded me on several occasions. Many times when he told me I should call him "Lord" I would say in my mind, "You should be called Nabal." (1 Samuel 25:3-42)

I began to pray about the situation between George and his boss. The boss could just call immigration, and we would all be sent back to St. Vincent without being able to pack our belongings. I asked the Lord to send someone to talk to George before he saw his boss. A good friend of ours who drove a taxi cab came by one night. He said he was about to go home when he saw a woman with a young child waiting for a taxi. He asked her where she was going to and the lady told him the area. The location she was going was not on the cab driver's route, but because it was late and for the sake of the child, he told her he would take her home. The lady lived on the same street as us; God sent the taxi cab driver that night. Since the man had been working all day, I went to the kitchen and made him a hot meal knowing that the meal would convince him to stay longer allowing him to talk for a while with the preacher. I left them alone and went to the bedroom to listen discreetly to their conversation.

Everything on my husband's mind came out to the taxi driver. George told him how he planned to confront the boss about speaking negatively about him and that he would offer the boss rent for the house. The brother from the church told him, "No, you can't do that. You will be putting your family in danger. You don't know what this man will do to you and your family. He can even call the police and tell them you stole things from him. I know of a brother in a church who is living not far from here. Let me ask him if you and your family can stay with him and his wife. They will most likely agree."

I went into the bathroom, knelt on the floor, and thanked the Lord for answering my prayer. That same week, we all moved to the taxi cab driver's brother's home. Even though we did not know the man and his wife, we all lived like a big happy family for a short time. Since the preacher was uncomfortable living in his sheepskin all the time, he moved us to a small shack.

Because we moved quickly, George did not have time to let his customers know that he was leaving the tailor shop. Some of his customers knew the boss, so he could not tell them fearing the boss would get angry. Now most of his customers were people from our church, but they did not pay their bills. They would bring half of the money most of the time, and the preacher would have to keep asking for the balance. Children of God, please be more trustworthy. You may not know the needs of the person you are short in paying, but God will also hold back on you if you hold back on your financial responsibilities. This can cause a lot of friction in families.

One day, I got a letter from my mom saying that our home in St. Vincent was about to be sold. The preacher went down on his knees and cried out, "Lord! Why are these things coming upon me?"

I looked at him crying and asked the Lord to give me a word and to let him listen to what I would say. I felt holy boldness arise within me as I walked over to my husband. I placed my hand on his shoulder, and he turned around. I looked him straight in the eyes and said, "Everything is going to be just fine. I'll call my mom and ask her to pay the money for the house. I know she will do it for you."

"Oh yes, that's a good idea! I can't see how the mortgage for the house went up so high. I asked my brother to take the rent money and pay it for me. That small head; that dirty snake!"

I stopped his ranting. "Let's not go there until we know the facts." That was the first time he had ever listened to me.

I called my mother to ask if she could help us and how much we owed. She told me the amount, plus she told me the people in the office said that the reason why it was for sale was that no money was paid on it for two years. My mom went on to say that she would pay for half and my sister Arlene would put up the other half. My younger sister had just begun to work as a nurse and had very little savings.

George was sitting next to me as I talked with my mom on the phone, but he did not ask to say hi to her. As soon as I put the phone down, he began to shout, "I know it. I know it. She loves me." He then asked me what my mother had said, and I told him that she said that Arlene and she would pay the money, but we would have to pay them back. "Oh yes," he said, "As soon as things get better."

Things did not get better but only got worse. The lady that visited him in the tailor shop came to visit with her child. I don't know how she found him or if he was the one to tell her where he was living.

We had limited cash, and whenever George got work, he never remembered the promise that he made to my mom. I told him that he could send a hundred dollars instead of buying new shoes for himself. His reply was "I never asked your mother for the money. It was you who asked."

As the months rolled by, he never sent any money to pay his bills. A letter came from the mortgage company stating that the house was up for sale again because no money was paid on the loan. After reading the letter, he ordered me to call my mother and tell her to pay the money. I reminded him about the money that he had never paid back to her. By this time, my mom was a widow and all she had to live on was the money from the banana field. I could tell George was getting angry with me, so I said, "Seeing as she loves you so much, why not call her yourself." His face lit up with a smile, and I walked away, leaving him to make his call and laughing in my heart.

Full of confidence he picked up the phone. I could hear his end of the conversation; he did not even ask how my mother was. He went straight to the point of asking for the money, and the conversation ended abruptly. I knew that things did not go his way.

"This is a conspiracy between you and your mother and sister because she has the money to pay for the house," he shouted at me. "They want it for themselves. Nobody is going to take my house. My father will not let anyone take that house from me; he is a strong wizard and will kill anyone who tries to hurt me. Tell your mother and sister to look out; he will send them mad."

For the rest of the day, he stayed in the bed and did not eat. I knew that he was planning something in his mind. Suddenly, he jumped up and said, "Yes, I have the answer! Come, come, let me tell you what we are going to do." I stood next to him, looking into his eyes as they changed from black to blood red. "Now, this is what we are going to do. The boat leaves every week to go back to St. Vincent. I can get on without anyone seeing me. You must not let anybody know that I'm not in Trinidad. When the boat reaches St. Vincent, I will get off without being seen. I will go up to your mother in the banana field. I know she will be alone. She will be harvesting the bananas. I will wait for her and kill her in the field. No one will suspect me. Getting back onto the boat is not a problem. By the time they find her body, I will be back in Trinidad."

I stood there looking at him and nodded my head in agreement with him. I feared that if I disagreed, I would not hear the rest of his plans. As he talked, he licked his lips from one side to the next. I tried to get rid of the lump in my throat by putting my head forward.

After explaining his plan, he called our daughter over and said, "Daddy has something very important to do. Don't tell anyone daddy is not home when I'm gone."

He came up with his plan on Friday, and the boat would be in Trinidad on Wednesday. I took the rest of those days to pray and fast. I knew that if I told my mother, she would not believe me because she trusted George over me. She could have even made things worse for all of us. I started praying for some money to give to George, thinking that maybe that would make him change his mind. The days slipped by, and there was no answer from God.

About seven o'clock Wednesday morning, I heard groaning coming from the bathroom. I stood in the kitchen and listened. The noise became louder, so I went to see what was going on. To my great surprise, I saw the preacher rolling from side to side in a fetal position. When I leaned over, he said, "I don't know what is going on. I think my boss sent evil for me."

"What are you talking about?"

He then pulled his pants down. I had to jump away because I had never seen anything like what I saw. With my hands at my mouth, I looked in astonishment at the swelling in his groin area.

"No one but my boss did this to me."

I knew that he knew the Bible from front to back, so I decided to talk in parables to him. "How can your boss do this to you knowing the devil can't touch a child of God? His hands have to be dirty with sin. You are a child of God, a preacher who prays for people and casts out evil spirits."

Then I left the room to give him time to think. I went outside to laugh; I wasn't laughing for what was upon my husband but at how the Lord had answered my prayer. God placed George in his bed to think. Now, he could not go to St. Vincent to kill my mother.

When I went back inside, I asked George if he wanted to go and see a doctor.

"I'm not going to let any woman look at me; I'm a man."

I told him that I would go to see the doctor and explain the situation, and he agreed. I spent half the day waiting to see the doctor and explain what was going on, but she told me she was unable to help my husband without seeing him. I pleaded with her telling her that he would not come. I told her that I wanted to sleep that night and he was rolling around in pain. She finally gave me medication for the pain and the infection that he may have.

"Tell him to drink plenty of water and to keep the area cool. This is something that men have when they are overheated. He must go and see a doctor because this can happen again."

It took two weeks before George was back to normal. He never went to a doctor. One thing I know is that he had a lot of time to think in those days as he was in the bed and could not move. I had to bathe him and bring everything to the bed for him, which I did willingly. He never spoke about going to St. Vincent to kill my mother again.

———◆◆◆◆———

I came to the point where I could rest in the arms of the Lord Jesus Christ. Whenever I was faced with anything that was too big for me, and everything is too big, I gave it to the Lord and watched Him make a way where there was no way. He is the same Jesus who said "I change not." So, what He did for the three Hebrew boys and Daniel in the lions' den, He can do for us today. If you do not know Him as your Savior, you only need to call on His name and then ask Him to cleanse your sins and abide in your heart. He will. For those of us who do know Him, He will do what He promised. Ask Him to give you a child-like faith. Jesus will make you laugh!

10
Old Wounds, Fresh Sore

Some wounds are healed with time, but there are some that time can't heal until the situation is dealt with. Many people will see me smile at times, but they don't know the inner wounds I carry each day. My wounds are internal; they travel from my heart to my womb and back again. This wound will not heal until all of my children are back in my life.

God has blessed me with four beautiful children. Yes, I said four. Many people who know me have only seen three. One girl and two boys, but it is not so; I have lived with this wound since my last pregnancy. Only God and the people who are involved know what took place.

During my last pregnancy, I had twins. The Lord showed me that someone was going to steal my baby, so I told my husband what the Lord had shown me and asked him if he could be with me in the hospital, just to let them see that I had someone. He looked at me with hate in his eyes and laughed while saying, "You are a mad woman!"

The day came that the doctor gave me to come in for surgery. A lady was in the bed next to me, and she went for her surgery first so her husband could be there when she woke up. When it was my turn to go in, a nurse asked if I had any standby blood. I told her that some people from the church had come and donated. My husband did not; he told me that he needed his blood. I was alone with the doctors and nurses with no husband at my side. Everyone had someone there except for me. Tears filled my eyes as I was about to be lifted from one bed to the surgery table.

I then clearly heard a voice saying to me, "I am here. Don't be afraid." I knew that voice was my only Friend, the same voice that would talk to me in the middle of the night. I whispered, "It's my Friend. It's my Friend." Then the mask was put over my face.

When I awoke, I was in a different room with other ladies. Still sleepy, I called to a nurse and asked her if my husband had come to visit. She said, "I did not see any male going to your bed. I was sitting here the entire time. Just a group of ladies came who said that they are from your church."

Visiting hours had been over for a long time when I heard my husband's voice asking for me. He walked over to me and asked me where the baby was. He wanted to see if the baby looked like him. The nurse told him that the baby was in the nursery. Off he went, and he came back with the same speed and said, "You have a boy."

He took off again, leaving me saying, "A boy is a boy, but where is the other child?"

After he was gone, another nurse came and asked me if I would sell my baby to her. "No," I told her. "I was told by different doctors that I was carrying twins, so where is the other baby?" I told her about the dream and how I had seen someone steal a baby girl from me.

This tall, dark iron-faced nurse with a protruding mouth bent over me and said, "If you say anything more, you will not leave this place alive."

Fear gripped me. My abdomen began to pain me so badly that I began to cry. The nurse walked away. A lady who was on the next bed close to me came over holding her belly. She said, "Let me hold the place that was cut. That may ease your pain." I drifted off to sleep but the pain never left me.

The next day I told my husband what was said to me by the nurse and that my baby daughter was missing.

"You are a mad woman, and I already told you that I am willing to take you to the mental institution."

My husband knew that several doctors had confirmed that I was pregnant with twins, which was enough reason to inquire about the other baby. But, what could I do since I did not have my husband's support?

About a year later, a man who came to visit us told us about the distress that he and his wife experienced at the same hospital. He said that after his wife had her baby, the nurse told him that the baby was dead. He then asked the nurse to show him the dead baby. The nurse told him she could not do so at the time but would do so the next day because the baby could not be found. The next day, he was shown a three month fetus and told that it was his baby. His wife had delivered after nine months. She saw the baby after birth and heard the baby cry, but she never saw the baby after that. A nurse took the baby out of the room, and then she came back to the room and told his wife that the baby was dead.

Three years later, I was in San Juan walking on the sidewalk with my youngest son holding my hand. A lady was walking towards us with a little girl. As the two children saw each other, they ran to the arms of each other and held on to each other as tight as they could. I stood there and said nothing. The lady tried to pull the little girl away but could not. When I asked, "What is going on here?" she pulled harder. I stood there looking at the children and was stunned by their resemblance. When I reached over to touch the little girl, the lady gave her a big tug, leaving the two children stretching their hands out towards each other. The lady increased her pace as she walked away. As my son and I stood there looking at them walking out of sight, I knew that the little girl was my baby and my son felt it too. When we got home, I told my husband what had taken place. He asked me if I had gotten the lady's name, and I told him "No." He smiled and that was the end of the conversation.

I wanted so badly to tell someone, but my husband thought that I was a mad woman and that he would have taken that situation and used it against me as he always did. Sometimes he would change things around, moving something from where I left it and then try to convince me that I was losing my mind when I began to search to locate it. I decided to stay quiet until the Lord shone some light into that deep dark wound.

<hr />

Because I would talk often with the Lord, He began to show me things that were about to happen, and my insecure husband would insist that it came from the devil. One of the gifts that the Lord has blessed me with is the discernment of spirits.

I can remember one Sunday when a couple attended our church. After my husband finished preaching, they stayed on for prayers. Everyone had left the church, except my family and the couple. I sent the children out to play, and as I sat there I knew I should remain silent as I had been taught by my husband. The lady was very quiet and reminded me of myself. The two men began talking.

"You see, Pastor, I do not have anything to feed my family with, and I cannot pay my rent. On Monday I have to attend the court because of a case pending. If only I can have a thousand dollars, it will cover everything."

As I sat there my thoughts went back to two days before when the Lord blessed me with one thousand dollars. I remembered praying for one thousand dollars to purchase a stove. While I had been praying, a woman, who was a member of the church, came running breathlessly and handed me the thousand dollars.

"I was just at home when I heard a voice telling me to go to the bank and withdraw one thousand dollars for you," she said to me. "I tried to ignore the voice but it would not go away. I dropped everything that I was doing at home and here I am. Take it! Take it! Now I am at peace with myself."

I told her that I was talking to the Lord about my need for a stove. She rejoiced because of the realization that the Lord had used her.

Our old stove was unserviceable, and I had to cook outside in the yard on three stones. The neighbors used my yard for a shortcut and often they would pass by and anxiously examine what was being prepared without my invitation.

As I sat on the bench that day in church behind my husband, I could sense that the Holy Spirit was saying that the man was on drugs and the lady was not his wife. I wrote what I sensed on a small piece of paper and passed it to my preaching husband. He read it, crumpled the note, and threw it on the floor. George told the man to come to our home during the week to receive the money.

My heart sank within me because I knew the money we had was my answer to prayer and my hope for a new stove was utterly destroyed. On our way home I told George that God sent that money to buy a stove. His reply was, "You only think of yourself." Later that week, he went ahead and gave the couple my one thousand dollars with no thought of how I felt.

The next Sunday he took the opportunity to exalt himself and his goodness. He told of how he gave a couple money, and he degraded me effortlessly. He told the congregation that it is hard to please the Lord when you have a wife not wanting you to do God's will. I could feel all eyes on me so I smiled as women in my culture do when embarrassed. At the end of the service I tried to hide myself, but I had nowhere to go.

This church that he had preached the sermon at was not our home church. He was assigned there for a three-month period. The following Sunday morning the pastor of the church called us into his office.

"Sit down, brethren, I have a problem to discuss with you. The couple that you spoke with last week…"

"Oh yes, Pastor!" my husband answered. "The man and his wife had some problems, so I did what the Lord would have me do."

The pastor looked at him, leaned forward, and said, "I heard that you gave one thousand dollars to this couple who also went to another church and asked for a thousand dollars. You see, my brother, you have overstepped your bounds. You should have spoken first with me because I know the man is on drugs and also living with a woman who is not his wife."

My preaching husband dropped his head, but I was not surprised because the Lord had already shown this to me. George's ego was deeply wounded. I did not say anything to the pastor at that time about what I knew, and we left and went home. I knew that if I mentioned anything concerning our meeting with the pastor, I would experience the fullness of George's rage and anger.

During the Sunday night service, I could not withhold my pain any longer. The worship service was in full swing, and people were just letting God have His way in their lives. I felt someone come and hug me firmly, yet gently. I began to cry and wail uncontrollably. I could not contain myself. The entire congregation was both shocked and amazed because I was always silent and unemotional. George was ministering to others, and a well-meaning saint suggested that he should pray for me at this time because I seemed to be in distress, but he dismissed the open evidence because he was ashamed. After a while, he came over and whispered in my ears, "Stop it. What is wrong with you?" I bawled even louder, so he walked away. Some sisters came and ministered to me.

That night when we entered our house he immediately became both physically and verbally abusive. He told me that I was nothing but a knife and not his wife.

From that day on, I began to speak to other pastor's wives, just to discover they also had secrets from behind the pulpit. For example, one pastor left his family to go abroad to preach and began a new family. The wife was too ashamed to speak out; she said to me that "No one would believe me because I am a minister's wife." Her words were the very words that I often heard from my own preacher husband – words meant to silence me permanently and to convince me that no one would believe my life's nightmare.

My main reason for keeping silent for all those years was because I saw lots of people being saved and lives being transformed by God. I would ask the Lord, "Why is this so? How can deception be in the pulpit?" The Lord reminded me that it is not man but His Word which cannot lie, and His Word would not return to Him void but accomplish what it was sent to do. Then I began to ask God, "When will you make a way for me out of this hell?"

Someone said to me I should keep quiet because George was instrumental in drawing a large crowd to the church. These comments reminded me of the tragedy that surrounded Jim Jones and his followers. I perceived that my husband's anger and controlling spirit might eventually spill over to his congregation. I decided that I needed to come forward and speak out in order to put a stop to things before they went way out of control.

My husband realized that I was slowly taking back my will, thinking on my own without telling him what I was thinking, and going out with no regard to his curfew. Sometimes I would just go out, buy an ice cream and sit for a couple of hours looking at people pass by. I knew what would happen when I returned home, but I did not care anymore.

I truly understood what the black slaves went through before they were freed. Many were beaten and killed; I was killed on the inside too. My emotions were dead. I could not cry, laugh, or love because my heart was hardened towards men and especially men behind the pulpit.

Mind you, I also knew some women whose husbands were preachers; these husbands would talk about their wives as the love of their lives. At first I did not believe it was true, so I went to their homes and asked the wives. I could see the love in their homes, even up to this day. One of those couples will be celebrating twenty-six years of marriage! I take my hat off to that man of God, and I know there are many more marriages like theirs, but they are hard to find.

I met an old couple once who told me that they went through their own time of war in their marriage. The old man remarked, "I just wanted to be one of the guys, so I went out drinking telling my buddies I was going home to give Helen (his wife) hell. I drunkenly sang all the way back home that someone is getting a beating tonight. When I arrived home, Helen was in bed sleeping, so I shouted at her for no reason at all. The innocent woman did me no wrong, and I hit her. She sprang up and retaliated. The next morning my face was swollen; I never laid a hand again on my sweet Helen."

Hearing this old man tell his story was so amazing that I doubled up with laughter. I asked Helen if it was true, and she replied that every word was true. I looked at the both of them standing there and laughing. He only had one upper tooth in his mouth, and she had none. This man is now blind, and his sweet Helen is taking care of him.

One night when George thought I was asleep, he went to the mirror and looked at himself. I wondered if he really treasured himself or if he was looking at himself with a mixture of pity and pain.

--- ◆•✕•◆ ---

Not one day would pass without George telling me that I was a crazy woman. At one point, I honestly felt like I was losing it; I would put an object down, and he would move it without me knowing it just to prove his point. When I asked him if he moved it, he would reply, "I told you I should take you to a mental institution."

One afternoon he asked me to go with him and a brother from the church to a mental asylum to pray for a sister. When we got there, he went quietly to nurse. I watched as they both turned and looked at me. He returned with a cunning smile on his face and said, "I was only asking the nurse the time for visiting hours." Of course, that was a big lie.

We went around the ward while he prayed for some people. As we were about to leave for home, he turned to me and said, "Seeing that you are here, you can sign yourself up as a patient."

I very quickly walked away from the hospital grounds as I didn't know if he had made plans for someone to capture me.

That day I finally knew my life was in great danger. I began to put the pieces of puzzle together. George always slept with a cutlass on his bed or under his pillow. Yet with all that was happening, he was still deeply involved in the church, preaching, living life, and telling people about their sins. My prayers became extremely intense toward God.

By this point, George had stopped eating food I prepared for him and cooked for himself because he didn't want me to touch any of the food he bought. I became a thief in my own home. I had to wait until he was not looking and steal his food. Since I wasn't working and couldn't buy my own food, I had no other way to eat. He told me if I worked that people would look at him as though he was not a man. That was just another means of controlling me.

One day, George caught me with his food and knocked it out of my hands. I went over to the home of a sister from the church and told her what was going on. In the beginning, she did not believe me because everyone was captivated by his charisma. I showed her the marks on my body, and, being overwhelmed with compassion, she cried and started calling out to God on my behalf. At one point I was jealous of her because she could cry and I could no longer cry because I didn't want to give George the satisfaction of seeing me crying. The sister gave me a few things to cook, and I took them home with me but I could not touch the stove that the pastor had given to us as a gift after had given away my thousand dollars away to the couple.

I had to wait until George was out of the house in order to touch anything in the home. Sometimes he would ask the children if I had touched anything in the house while he was gone. After using utensils, I would be sure to wash and put them back exactly as he had left them. At times, I would fan the television to cool off before he got back home, so that when he touched it, it would appear to be just as he left it.

The situation became worse between us, and I could not look at him. If our eyes met, he would quarrel and speak to himself continuously for half of the day. When he realized that I preferred to not be drawn into his intended conflict, he stirred up the children and encouraged them to degrade me through labeling.

My youngest son was just learning to form sentences, and the first sentence he learned to repeat to anyone that visited the home was "My mother is an insubordinate wife." He had no clue of what he was saying. It was like a song sung in his ears each day by his father. Anytime I went out and returned with things for the children to eat, my husband would throw the things away and tell the children that I picked it up on the streets.

One morning, George said some obscene words to me, and a few hours later I asked him if he wanted a mango. He turned to me and said, "You are like Sarah in the Bible; the only thing is you don't call me 'Lord.'" I just looked at him and smiled. He never understood how I could continually speak kindly to him.

At that time, George had no idea I was about to leave him. He was making plans to visit an old girlfriend in St. Vincent. He had heard that the lady, whom he spoke about for the past fifteen years of our marriage, was single again. He said the first thing he had to tell her was he was sorry that they did not get married. I just looked at him and smiled. He thought I was a fool. I was not going to stay and play any love triangle with them.

I chose to use my God-given brains rather than my mouth against my husband. I can remember just a few houses away from where we had lived in St Vincent there was a lady who was abused by her common-law husband. Many times I would see him hopping on his one leg with a weapon in his hand trying to get at her. I knew if he had not been one-legged, she would have been a dead woman long before. The lady confided in a friend about her intentions to leave her husband forever. That so-called friend went back and told the husband about his wife's plans. Never let your plans to leave your abuser become known to him.

I woke up one morning to see a group of people in front of the couple's gate. The husband had stabbed his wife while she slept, and she died immediately. Their children heard nothing because they slept soundly. The husband tried to get rid of the body but was unsuccessful because of his physical limitation. He asked his brother to help him. They took the body to the hospital, pretending that she did not die at home. When they arrived at the hospital with the body, the hospital refused to listen to their story and advised them that the hospital is for the sick, not those who were dead for hours. The doctor refused to touch the body, demanded that they remove it from the room, and then called the police. That lady left four children without parents.

We must remember that there is a real devil out there, and lots of women are married to his sons. Demons may try to inhabit the bodies of humans; they can't read our mind, but they can put evil thoughts in, and as soon as we open our mouths, they know what is in our heart. That's why the Word of God says to resist the devil and he will flee. The devil comes and plays on our emotions, and an uncontrolled tongue will not help us. It will destroy.

Have you ever felt trapped in your own body? I did. Somewhere inside was a voice wanting to be heard. Each time I wanted to break out, limited belief spoke persuasively to stay in where I belonged. I found myself going deeper into that dark hole. The hardest thing was I actually knew that I was in a deep dark hole, but no one seemed to see me as a victim. Sometimes I felt like I was choking; the very God-given air that is so abundant and free was being taken away. My life was slipping slowly; even my pretended smile was fading. No one took me serious. They thought that I just wanted to discredit a man of God. I was told that I was jealous of him. Our voices can easily go unheard, and the loudmouthed bully can seem more powerful. The bully gains his strength by sucking the life out of his victims.

I remember going to church on a Sunday morning and listening to the pastor call all who had a need to the pulpit for prayer. When the pastor saw me, our eyes met, and he walked to the back of the church to secure himself from his embarrassment. I guess when he saw me his conscience was awakened. The pastor was the same man I went to with blood running down my face after George had terribly abused me, and I was bleeding and swollen in different places. I asked myself, "Who can I turn to for help?" I felt even more trapped.

11

The Great Escape

God does not give us more than we can bear but always makes a way of escape. I clung to that thought as I decided to make the situation of my abuse known to a sister from another church.

She was one of my prayer partners and also the choir director of the children's choir of her church. Plans were being made for the choir to perform in Canada and the United States of America. The children in the choir were between three and sixteen years of age. I set out to assist the group by making and selling delicacies at schools in order to raise funds for the trip. I never had the slightest thought that I would be helping myself also.

After months of collecting the necessary funds, we were able to purchase the tickets. I went as usual that day to the sister's home for our time of prayers. After we finished our prayer session, she asked me if I would like to accompany the choir on the trip with all expenses paid. It was like a dream come true. On the way back home, I thanked God for the offer He sent my way. "This is my escape," I thought to myself. I finally saw a way out of my marriage hell.

I knew that if I told George about the offer, he would definitely say no, so I decided not to let him know my plans and instead used my God-given brains. I gave my passport to someone to keep safe for me. I then asked God for wisdom to be able to escape without George's awareness.

About one week before the trip, I told him I was going to accompany the choir to Canada and the United States of America. He made no reply, proceeded towards the bedroom, and locked the door behind him. I heard papers ruffling and drawers slamming, and I knew he was searching for my passport to burn it just as he had done with all my red-colored clothes. That night he was very silent. He couldn't locate my passport in his bedroom, so he assumed it must be in the children's room and he searched there. The following day he continued his search in every area of the house with no success. I pretended that I was unaware of what was going on.

Each day George made remarks to me, calling me "a stupid woman." He never realized I was putting out dead bait to catch a live fish because most of the time I was playing dumb just so he would remain oblivious of my mental capabilities.

When George finally realized that he was unsuccessful in locating my passport, he asked, "How long will this trip be and when are you leaving?" I gave him the date as two months ahead, when really it was just one week before our departure date.

Somehow I believe he made his own inquires about the date and time of the trip because on the day that I was leaving he began loudly exclaiming that he despised the fact that I was invited to go on the trip. He then drew his cutlass and demanded that I say something in reply to his comments. I hurriedly gathered what clothing I had left that he had not burned, threw the clothes into a sack, pulled the strings, slung the sack on my back, kissed my youngest son goodbye, and ran out of the house and down the steep hill – all without looking back.

I hitched a ride to the airport. The entire time I was in a trance-like state and totally unaware of my emotions. When I reached the terminal, I repeatedly looked over my shoulders expecting to see my husband creating a big uproar as was his usual custom.

We boarded the plane at two in the afternoon, and my heart was very heavy because I had left my children behind to suffer the consequences of my actions. My only comfort was remembering what Jesus said to his disciples – "If I do not go, the Comforter would not come." I had to practice tough love. I was leaving to make a better life for my children.

While my heart was heavy, I knew it was God's timing for me to leave because a brother in the church shared with me that George said he was thinking about killing me.

Our time in Canada was great, but I was very anxious. I prayed each day asking God to provide a home and a way for me to stay.

12

God Answers Prayers

During the last week while preparations were being made to return to Trinidad, I asked God if He wanted me to return to the same situation back home. The Lord had already done His part in getting me out of the country. The door was there; I just had to open it and walk through. I made inquiries at the church hosting the choir to find out if anyone needed a babysitter. Just three days before our departure, the pastor informed me that his wife was in the process of looking for a babysitter and promised he would discuss my offer with her and would give me an answer the next day.

That night I received no sleep, and I prayed all night asking God to let me find favor with a lady who had not yet interviewed me. The next day before the service began, I received my answer. The pastor's wife approached me and remarked that God had sent me at the right time. I got the job, and, for the first time that night, I really heard the sweet voices of the children's choir. I sang and danced with joy and jubilation.

After the service, I told the choir director that I had accepted a job and would remain in Canada. She was both surprised and shocked and asked me what I intended to do about my children. I responded by telling her that I was doing this for their benefit.

The night before the departure of the choir, I sat down and wrote some letters to my children and gave them to different people to be posted in Trinidad within a certain time period. One of the letters was placed in a bag with some things for my children. I did this to throw off my husband so that he would think that I had returned to Trinidad.

I heard later that when he realized I had not come home, he went looking for me at every sister's home that he knew and shouted in the streets, "You have my wife in there. Send her out!" He even said to one of them that he had a vision I was living on a hill and hiding out at her home, hoping that the sister would confess to him; but all the while I was in Canada.

By this time I had worked three months at my job with the pastor and his family. I quickly realized the wife was unhappy, but I could not put a finger on the source. Often I would hear the pastor shouting at her even though she was a hard-working woman who loved her husband and children.

This pastor knew the words in the Bible but never applied the Word to his life. Each day I was attacked by him. He would either press himself against me or inquire about my sexual life in Canada although he knew I was not sexually active. On Sundays while riding with the family to church, if I ever glanced at the rearview mirror, it seemed that his eyes were on me. I tried to change seats with one of the sons, but the father ordered him to remain in his usual assigned spot.

One day the pastor came home from work early with the wrong intentions. He asked how I felt, not having had sex for such a long time. I told him I didn't need any man to have sex with because God designed sex for a man to have with his own wife or a woman with her own husband. I thought to myself, "I wonder what he really sees when he looks in the mirror? Would he see his own reflection or that of an animal?" Funny enough, one can look at some men and see the actions of an animal. How does the world see us? Can we look into the mirror of life and see a good reflection? We are what we do, not what we say, as words are easy to come by.

Naturally, the atmosphere in the house was harsh since I had just escaped from an abusive relationship. The following day, the pastor arrived home early again and told his little son to go to his room and play. I sensed what was next – the same questions as the day before. When he recognized pursuing the matter was useless, he ended our conversation by saying, "I know you will not have sex with anyone but your husband, so I am going to ask my wife for a divorce and marry you."

I was shocked and answered, "No, I am not a home wrecker."

Later that night his wife confided in me that after having sex, her husband asked her for a divorce. She also told me she suspected he had another woman at his workplace.

During the nights I would pull my bed behind the bedroom door so that the pastor could not enter my room. When he realized what I was doing, he told his wife to inform me that I should not move around the furniture. One night I took ten empty cans and put them behind the door. At midnight there was a big crash – he was trying to get in. I do not know why his wife never heard the noise because the children were alarmed out of their sleep and ran in the direction of the noise. I sometimes wondered if he had drugged his wife because he usually gave her a glass of juice before bedtime.

The next day everyone was up and about, but not a word was said about the noise until we were around the dining table. One of the boys swallowed what he had in his mouth and started saying, "Last night…," when before another word could come forth, his father intervened and told him to leave the table at once. The son was just about to reveal to his mother all she had missed the previous night.

The following Sunday at church, I informed the senior pastor of what had been happening to me in the house. To my amazement, he laughed at me! He told me that the pastor was only joking since he was a jovial person and that I should not leave because of that. I was very hurt and disappointed in this senior pastor. I then asked myself, "Didn't God put him here to feed and protect the sheep?" From that point on, I pleaded with God to make a way out of the situation.

On a different Sunday, two sisters approached me after the service and inquired about what was wrong. One of them pointed out that I usually had a smile on my face, but my smile was no longer there. I enlightened them about the situation, and that same week they made arrangements for a taxi to pick me up and drive me to their home at three in the morning while everyone slept.

The taxi driver was given someone else's address a few doors away, so I had to get there in time to stop the driver from ringing someone else's doorbell. I was unable to take many of my belongings, so I put a few things in a bag and walked out of the pastor's home very quietly. The taxi driver took me to the sister's home. One of the sisters was a spinster while the other was married. The husband of the married sister cared for me as his daughter, and he was among the few Christian men I had met who lived with integrity and according to godly principles. They were all concerned for me and showed me extreme respect and love.

Later on, I got a job as a live-in babysitter, but it was another unhealthy situation. At times I would work for the entire week without receiving any salary. I was spat on, cursed and even locked out in the winter by my employer and her children. In the area where my job was located, no buses ran the streets and the houses were far apart. At one point, when I was locked out in the snowy cold, I wanted to give up and lie down on the side of the road, but I remembered my children who I had left back home and was comforted by the hope of seeing their faces again. With many prayers, I mustered up some strength and walked to the closest house. When I arrived, the door swung open revealing a little Italian lady standing there with a blanket. She was already dressed to set out to meet me. She told me she saw me coming but I was taking so long to get there that she thought that I would never make it. She handed me a hot cup of tea, but my frozen hands prevented me from holding it, so she held it to my mouth and fed me. One thing I can say is that God's eyes were always upon me regardless of the situation that I found myself in. He proved to always be there to make a way of escape.

13

Determination

As the weeks went by, I held on to the fact that after the darkest hour, dawn always breaks through. I was determined not to return to Trinidad and more dark days. What I did not know was that I was entering into my darkest hours of not knowing where I would sleep on the weekends.

I caught chicken pox from the children in the home where I babysat and lived during the week. My entire body was covered in sores, even my tongue. The bottom of my feet felt as though I was walking on sharp pointed objects. I had no one to put the lotion on my back, and I felt as though a thousand army ants were walking on me. I cried myself to sleep for the entire week. Because I was sick, one of the Jamaican sisters asked that I not come home for the weekend. Since I had nowhere else to go, I asked my employer if I could stay for the weekend. She agreed but asked me to stay in my room because she did not want her guests to see me.

Three weeks later I asked one of the sisters if it was alright for me to come home for the weekend. She inquired if all my sores were gone, and I told her, yes, only the marks were left. However, having just the marks was not good enough for her, and she told me I was not welcome to return home yet. My employer also told me I was not permitted to stay for the weekend, so I took some clothes, collected my pay, went to the mall, and sat there. As I watched people pass by, some smiled, and I did the same. I also prayed, "Lord, you have to send someone to take me in tonight."

Eventually, an old man about the age of seventy came and sat next to me. He couldn't speak English well, but I made out a few words. He told me how he was living on the streets with his son and that his wife was in India. He then said he needed someone to have sex with and went on to describe intimate details about the type of woman he wanted. Then he inquired about the spots on my skin and asked me if I had ever taken an AIDS test. I sat there in astonishment and stared at the old man for about ten minutes before he walked away.

I realized I knew how Job in the Bible felt with his children, money, and health taken away from him, and then the devil sent people to mock him. As it was getting dark, I started walking back to my employer's house planning in my mind what to say to her. I missed my bus, but just then a white van pulled up alongside me. A lady called out for me to receive a gospel tract and asked if I would like a ride to my home. I told her that I didn't have a home and had no idea where I was going to sleep for the night.

She told me that I could stay at her home with herself and her husband. I had no idea that she was a pastor's wife and was just grateful for a place to stay. On Sunday she took me to church in a building they rented just for Sunday services. The church only had five members, so the pastor's wife seemed very glad to have me there.

On Monday morning, I returned to work, and on the weekend the pastor's wife took me to her place again. Our routine went on for a couple of weekends until one Sunday morning when the pastor's wife told me that I should give her all of my salary to help pay for the use of the church building. I told her I could not put up my entire salary, but that I was willing to give an offering. She became very upset and told me she could no longer pick me up on weekends. So, the kindness of the pastor's wife ended, and I was once again without a place to stay.

By this time the spots on my skin cleared up, so I called one of the sisters and let them know that I was alright and would like to come down for the weekend. I also left my job as the live-in babysitter, because my employer was becoming increasingly angry, and I feared being reported to the authorities.

14

Bittersweet Hot Waters

I moved from one province to another before settling with a sister I had met upon my arrival in Canada with the children's choir. This sister was well known in her church as the song leader of the ladies choir and a mother of six children – three boys and three girls. Two of the children had already left home, and the mother was divorced and single caring for her other four children. The youngest daughter was fourteen years old, and we became close friends. She often confided in me because of her mother's frustration and negative attitude.

My stay at this sister's home was a bittersweet experience. I worked as a live-in babysitter in another home, but would spend the weekends with this family. Every Sunday morning and evening we all went to church because the mother was a very active member. Each weekend, I gave the mother one hundred and fifty dollars, but before I left at the end of the weekend, I would be without money because she would ask for additional money as a loan to pay her bills.

One Friday, as I was preparing to leave my place of employment and go down to her place for the weekend, the phone rang. I answered it and was told to not spend any of my salary. She wanted me to bring my money straight to her because she had a lot of bills to pay. This lady was receiving financial assistance from the children's father, from the church that provided her with a house, and from her own full-time job. Yet, all of that income was not enough for her.

One day she told me that I needed a man in my life. Naturally, I asked her "why" and "for what?" I was still carrying wounds from my marriage to George. She paid no attention to me and went on to tell me how she ran into an old school friend who was doing well and that I should date him. I did not know that she had already taken money from the man as an assurance for sex.

On one particular night, this rough, tall, black, fat man came to the house. After she introduced us, she sent the children to their rooms. The man proceeded to make advances towards me, so I told him not to touch me. When he didn't listen, I walked away and went to the bedroom which I shared with the fourteen-year-old daughter.

Shortly afterwards, the mother stormed into the room and, while pointing her fingers at me, raged, "You cannot treat my friend like that in my house because that is a nice man I set up for you. Everyone in the church is having sex, which world are you living in? Are you a praying mantis? Every spare minute you are down in the basement praying! Look around, you don't have anyone in case something goes wrong with you!" She then beat on her chest and continued, "I am well-off if I die tonight in the Lodge. I will see to it that my children have money. I have already joined my oldest son, so you see, we are fine, and I am just trying to help you."

I learned that this sister was having an affair with one of the men in the church. After church they would meet in an empty car park and use one of their cars to have sex in. She seemed proud to tell me this and also of the length of the affair. One day I overheard her and the guy quarreling, and she became very upset with me. He wanted some money back, and she didn't want to return it. Instead she ended up convincing her daughter to have sex with him. She handed him the daughter's picture to place in his car and then gave her daughter to him.

Then, after church the next Sunday, the sister introduced me to an old silver-haired man by saying, "This is the girl I told you about. You can have her, but I need you to buy me some fish every Saturday."

The old man smiled and looked me over from head to toe.

Her actions confirmed to me that it was time for me to leave her house. I decided to do so secretly, but before I left, I went to the pastor of the church and brought his attention to what she had done to me and her daughter. The pastor listened and responded, "If you don't like it there, then you should move."

To my knowledge, that's all he ever said about the matter. He never spoke to the sister about her actions, and she remained the unmarried choir director. I left that church and the sister who wanted to be my pimp.

One thing I continued to pray to the Lord was "You have brought me this far and will take me even further. Just let me live and give me the strength and health to go on." Even though people took my money, I still had the strength to go on. I left my live-in babysitting job at the same time because I did not want the church sister calling the immigration department and reporting me.

15
From the Pot to the Fire

The new family in another province that employed me next was a dysfunctional family. The father and mother continually fought and blurted out obscene words to each other and their two children, a girl of seven years and a boy of nine. And, instead of Mrs. Mars returning from work to attend to her children, she would go to bars or clubs with her friends. I started having pain behind my neck, not knowing it was stress related because I was the only one to care for the home and children.

The boy, who was the older child, was okay as long as he was allowed to watch the television. His mother often asked if I assisted him with his schoolwork and I had to tell her that as soon as I mentioned schoolwork to him, he would take the nearest thing to him and launch it at me.

One afternoon the children asked for hot cocoa, and I sat at the table as we all drank. I told the son that after dinner I would help him with his homework and that he could watch cartoons or whatever he wanted to after that. Suddenly I felt a hot liquid in my face. The boy had thrown his cup of hot cocoa in my face. I picked up the phone and called his grandma. Her reply was "You know what he is like. Don't worry about him. He is just looking for attention."

At about seven o'clock that evening, I took the girl upstairs for her bath so that in the morning before school all she would have to do is freshen up. I was completely startled when she cleared her throat, turned and spat in my face, and slammed the door as she left the bathroom. I went to my room and cried. They knew the law. I could do nothing to discipline them. At nine-thirty that night, while the children were downstairs watching television, I went to my window and drew back the blinds to see outside. I watched the heavy blowing snow with flakes looking like large cotton candy pieces. I continued watching until the flakes vanished from the windowpane and my mind was off of the earlier episodes of the evening.

I didn't realize how long I stood at the window, and it was eleven o'clock before I stepped away. I went to the children's room, but no one was in bed. They were still downstairs sitting in front of the television. I told them that I heard their father's car pulling up the driveway in order to get them in bed without my having to be at the receiving end of things being thrown.

The following day the son's teacher sent his mother a letter with a smiley face sticker on the envelope. He was so happy that he didn't want me to touch it, and he placed it in his mother's room. The next morning, Mrs. Mars stormed into my room, pulled me out of my bed, and said, "This cannot go on. I am paying you to take care of my children, which you don't." (I was receiving seventy-five dollars per week and sometimes less.) She showed me the letter from her son's teacher:

"Dear Mrs. Mars: Is everything okay at home with your son? He never seems to settle down in class. I often have to let him sit alone so that the other children can work. He has also never brought his homework to school completed. His excuse is that he didn't have time. What work are you giving him at home to do?"

Before I could finish reading, Mrs. Mars yanked the letter from my hand and directed some strong obscene language at me.

That morning, I got the children ready for school and walked them to the bus stop. Upon returning to the house, I quietly walked up the stairs just in time to hear Mrs. Mars on the phone asking someone if they knew the number for the immigration office. After she left for work, I heard a strange car pull up in the driveway and fear washed over me. The person who got out of the car had on a winter jacket with the hood pulled up, and I couldn't see a face. When the knocking started, my heart pounded so hard it felt like it was falling out of my chest. I peered through the peep-hole only to find it was covered with snow. I glanced out the side window to see that it was one of my employer's friends.

I quickly opened the door for the friend, and, as she entered, she stared me straight in the eyes and said, "I'll come to the point, you have to get out of here right now! That mad woman who is my friend has asked me for the number of the immigration office to call and report you. I have seen how hard you worked with her children, and I wish that you were my children's sitter." She then handed me a slip of paper with one of her friend's numbers who was living in another province. "Call her now. I have already told her about you. My friend is living alone and would be happy to have company."

"What will happen to the children when they return from school?"

"Let the grandfather take care of it. I will write a letter pretending to be you and say that you have run off with an African man. That will stop them from searching for you."

16

The Unknown

Once again, I was on my way to the unknown with my clothes packed in a plastic bag. The directions to the lady's house sounded quite easy, but I missed my first stop, and the bus driver did not have the courtesy to explain to me where I was. Finally, I reached the home of the lady's friend and was welcomed with open arms. Since I had no other job, I spent some time helping her in her home.

A few months later, I went out on my own for the first time and rented a room from a Filipino couple who owned a large, beautiful home. By this time I had saved up some money and was able to afford the $375 per month for rent. The wife was not a Christian, but she had the qualities of a godly woman, except for the fact that she stole some of my belongings.

When the wife cooked, she made sure that I had a very big plate of food to eat. I suggested my contributing money to the food, but she wouldn't allow it. Instead, I would bring home a lot of food stuff and ask her to help me eat it. When anyone visited her home, she would tell them that I was her daughter. I finally felt appreciated and free with my own room and keys!

However, when nighttime set in, I was unable to sleep because my mind and heart were with my children back in Trinidad. Whenever I saw the behavior of the children I babysat, I began to regard my own children as saints and would drift off thinking about them. The questions would always come to me: Have they eaten? Are they crying? I know they are in pain, I also am. In order to fall asleep each night, I played music on my headset and danced until I threw myself down on the bed and closed my eyes. Once I tried using some sleeping pills, but was still sleepy the following day. With dancing, I had no negative side effects.

I often asked God to have mercy on my children. My prayer was "Let not the sins of their father pass down to them." Many people think I am a bad mother to have left my children and go away. Even God knows tough love. I did not want my children to continually witness daily abuse and violence towards me by their father. If it had been possible to take my children along with me, I would have done so without a second thought, but I had absolutely no choice in the situation. I have tried on several occasions to obtain custody of them without any luck. I love them with all my heart and my arms are open and waiting for them.

Each day my heart aches for my children because George holds them ransom in order to bring pain and hurt to me. Without a doubt I know that he does not care about them. If he really did, he would not continue to utter awful words to them about me. I frequently heard him say to our oldest son that women are worth nothing and are to be used. Both of my sons need to know that women are a gift from God, and women are to be loved, respected, and appreciated. They need to know to never use their strength to overpower a woman but to protect her so that they will become strong men, not strong fools.

One day the lady I was staying with received a letter from my husband. When I had written to my children, he took the address and wrote a letter to the lady I was staying with at the time. As he often said, all women are fools, so he expected that by writing, he could arouse fear and motivate her to send me back to Trinidad. He tried to manipulate her mind, but it did not work.

Hi Mrs./Miss Judith S,

Greetings to you in Jesus' wonderful name. I, the husband of Ruth, felt led of the Lord to write to you to try at what appears to be the last effort to understand what has become of my wife. My wife and I had some problems, but that is not the real reason why she is there or hasn't come back home. I don't know who you are and what to tell you at this time.

Please tell me a little about yourself; send a picture, and I will send one of mine to you. I'm trying to recover my wife. The truth is, I don't even know if she is alive and what condition she is in. I would like to say I did not do the things my wife said I did. In the next letter, I'll explain to you in detail, but for now I just want to initiate lines of communication. Are you a Christian? Do you love the Lord? Then please do right so that blood won't be on your hands. Let me explain what I mean by blood on your hands. One, if you are party to what is happening, you could do something to stop or change my relationship instead of helping to save my marriage. Do know you will be judged by God and will be responsible for the destruction of this family? Selma also will be damaged by this. We have been married for sixteen years and had a good marriage. Our neighbors are witness; I can give names. The problem is not so much with you as it is with my wife Ruth. If you are a wise person, you will try to find out what really is the problem. Listen, observe, ask questions that you think are appropriate, then make your own conclusion. My children and I, her husband, are worried sick and very disappointed about her behavior, to rather go and live with their aunt in the States then to come to Canada. Their feeling is that their mother is very unstable, very spiteful and has abandoned them. This is harmful to both herself and them. If you are a Christian and know the story of Jonah, you will know that there will come a time that you will either be put off the ship or have your ship wrecked. Don't be partakers of other people's sin or God will judge your whole house. (Romans) I'm not trying to scare you but alert you of what God will have you know. He will first have warned. Please comply with God or face his wrath. Judge what I am saying and make your choice. All for now until I hear from you. Thank you for your reply.

Yours Respectfully,
George S.

One day after struggling for many nights to sleep, I thought to myself that if I went back to night school, my homework would take my mind off worrying about the children. I couldn't lose – I would be obtaining credits that I needed in order to receive a high school diploma. So, I went to night school and received excellent grades. I even got honors!

The world was no longer a scary place for me. I was able to interact with people around me. Once I had my high school diploma, I went on to secure other qualifications.

17

The God of Second Chances

With much prayer and fasting, I asked God to take away my desire for companionship even though I was very lonely in my new country. I prayed to the Lord, "I have you, Lord. What more do I need? I mean it, Lord. I don't want a desire for sex because I don't want a man in my life."

Two days later the pastor of the church I attended came up to me and said, "Do not shut out what God has for you, Ruth. You are a young, attractive lady." I scornfully laughed out loud as the pastor walked away. He had seen many young and old men try to pursue me, but I was not responding to them.

Months later I was walking through the mall and decided to enter a store just to look at the beautiful items. I touched the things I loved. I uttered prayer of praise thanking the Lord for a dress and skirt. Then I went into the underwear department. My eyes lit up at what I saw. "O Lord, thank you for the money to buy pretty panties. You know I can't buy these things without your help."

A still, small voice came back to me. "Your husband will buy you all these things."

"Lord, I am divorced. I don't have anyone but you."

Again the voice responded, "Just wait and see."

I stood there contemplating what was happening and prayed, "God, if you want me to have a husband, he must not have any mother, father, sister, or brother, and no in-laws. And, by the way, he must be in his late fifties. No more young men in my life." In my mind I thought this was a very tall order and God would have a hard time finding someone to meet my qualifications. I figured I had lots of time.

One year later I dreamed that I was on the beach taking a walk and enjoying the beauty all around. The sea waves came rolling to the shore then rolled back to the sea. I could hear sea birds in the air and watched some dive into the water. Up ahead of me was a tall man walking alone on the sand. I don't know what drew my attention to look at him, but I told myself that I must see the face of this man. From the back I could only see his long skinny legs in a pair of blue jeans, his light colored shirt, and his shoulder length hair. I walked faster. I was two steps behind him when a wave came ashore. I took some water in my hand and threw it on his legs, but he did not turn around. So, I walked faster ahead of him. After reaching a good distance in front of him, I looked back. I saw his blue eyes, the wind blowing his hair across his cheeks and then back away from his face again. He did not even see me looking at him. He was in his own world. He then walked off into a beautiful garden next to the beach.

A year later in August I was walking home from my babysitting job around four-thirty in the afternoon. The day was hot. I was wearing a black pair of fitted jeans and a green spandex top. My hair was combed back in a black ban-do and reached the middle of my back with the ends are curl under. Walking and checking the time on my watch for the arrival of the next bus, I started to cross the street. Just as my feet touched the pavement, I heard a loud truck horn. I glanced around to see a truck parked at the back of a store loading dock across the street. I noticed a hand waving. I looked over my shoulder to see if the person was waving at me or someone else.

The person shouted that he was waving at me. I wondered who he was since I didn't know anyone with a truck. As I walked closer, I saw the man was handsome and about six foot three inches with a beautiful smile. I approached him and shouted, "What is your problem? What do you want?"

With a soft voice, he said, "I just saw a lovely lady and wanted to say hi."

I shouted "hi" back to him and walked away. I had only one thing on my mind – how much time did I have to reach the bus stop. I reached the bus just before the door closed.

The next day at the same time, the same truck horn blared, and the man motioned for me to come over. I told myself that I would fix him good this time! I walked up to him, but before I could utter a word, he stretched out his hand to give me a piece of paper.

"Here is my phone number. Can I have yours?"

I took the paper, placed it in my hand bag, and walked away. I promised myself not to walk on that street again.

Weeks went by when one day I was looking through my hand bag for a bus ticket. I pulled out a piece of paper and saw a phone number. Then I remembered the truck guy. I heard a voice in my head encouraging me to give him a call.

After I found a seat on the bus, I pulled out my cell phone and dialed the phone number.

"Hello? Hello?"

Not knowing what to say, I said, "Hi, truck guy. Remember me? Black jeans and green top."

He laughed. "How could I forget? How are you? I look for you every afternoon."

He then asked if he could see me the next day, so I said I would see him at the same time and place.

The next afternoon I asked myself what I was doing crossing the street to meet this truck guy. As I got closer, I tried to smile but my heart was not in it. He stepped out of the truck with a smile on his face.

"Hi! My name is Andrew."

I shook his outstretched hand and introduced myself. I asked him where his place of birth was and discovered he was from Jamaica.

"Where are you living?" he asked.

"That is for me to know."

"Do you think we could go out sometime soon?"

His question raised my defenses. "Go out with you? If I go out with you and you try to touch me, I will break your hands." Andrew was six foot three inches and weighed about two hundred pounds. I know he saw in my eyes that I meant what I said.

"All I want is to have some fun. I don't kiss or have sex outside of marriage. I'm not looking for a wife, but I have a friend who is looking for a wife. Give me your number and I will give it to him."

We talked for a few minutes and then I went on my way to the bus stop.

Two weeks went by and I did not hear anything from Andrew. Somehow I was not surprised because I knew in my heart that all men are just out for one thing. If he thought he could have fun with me, let him think again.

A month later, Andrew finally called. He apologized for not getting back to me, and then he said he did talk to his friend at work about me, and the friend wanted to meet me. I told him it would have to be in a public place. We agreed to meet at a local coffee shop Monday morning.

I didn't know why I felt the pull to go ahead with our meeting, but I did. When I entered the coffee shop, a crowd of people was eating and laughing and all the tables were full. I stood in the doorway looking for Andrew. Finally I spotted a hand waving at me to come over.

Seated with Andrew was a man with his back to me. I could see his shoulder length hair. When I walked up to the table, the man stood up as Andrew said, "This is the chick I told you about."

I was completely shocked to be face to face with the same man from my dreams. He had the same blue eyes and blue jeans. Since my mind was racing back to my dream, I did not hear his name.

Andrew told us he had to go to work and left us alone to talk.

The man from my dream introduced himself again – his name was Mike. He told me he lived down the street. For about an hour, we sat there and talked. I told him how long I was living in Canada, that I was divorced and had children, and that I was from a large family.

"Well," Mike said, "I do not have a father, mother, sister, brother, or aunt. Only a dog. No one else but just me alone."

In my mind I thought, "This can't be!"

Mike did most of the talking, and then he surprised me by saying, "I would like to marry you." To my own surprise, I agreed!

He offered to show me where he was living, and on the drive to his place, I made sure he understood my standards. I told him that I did not have sex outside of marriage. He was very pleasant and said that he could wait. He wasn't one of those men who have to see it, touch it, and test it first.

His apartment was clean and nice. Everything I had asked God for was in that apartment plus more. We spent about twenty minutes looking around the apartment, and then it was time for me to get the bus. Mike wanted to drive me home, but I needed some time alone to take in all that was happening.

While sitting on the bus, I began to see how I asked God for something and He gave it to me and more. I had never come across anyone who did not have any family, but I asked for it thinking that God would have a hard time filling in my request. I was wrong.

Mike and I married the next year in January, but I had a hard time giving myself to him because of trust and my past. I had no desire for sex. One day I asked the Lord why I couldn't give myself to my husband and feel good about it. God reminded me about my prayer years before asking Him to take away any desire for sex. I remembered and asked the Lord to replenish my desire because Mike was very good to me. When God gives, He gives the best.

Two months later my husband filed for my landed papers, and I am now a Canadian happily living with my husband and dog.

18

Stolen Identity

Many people labeled me as a rebel over the years, but I am certainly not. I am a free woman who is now walking in my God-given liberty.

Some women seem to be non-existent and to lose their identity, respect, and self-esteem because people focus on the husband as the most important person, instead of the both the husband and wife as a whole. When a couple marries, sometimes the wife is no longer addressed as Mary, Margaret, or Sally but as Mr. Smith's or Brother Tim's wife. George always introduced me by saying, "This is my wife." A lot of people didn't realize I had my own name, and I was viewed as George's property, not an individual. I knew I had my own name along with a personality to match, but I was not allowed to show any God-given talents around my preacher husband. He would do his best to stop me from showing my talents to others too.

God blessed me with a talent for writing poems, but I dared not let George know that I wanted to recite one in the church because he would determine that I should put the poems away until "the right time." I would think of the parable about the servant whom the master gave one talent to invest, but the servant buried the talent and did nothing with it. When the master returned and found out the servant's actions, he called the servant wicked and took away the talent to give to the one with ten talents. This parable assured me that God didn't want me to bury my talents, yet George wanted me to bury my talents because he said I wanted to steal his show. To me, church is not a show but a place to grow and to glorify God with our talents.

Women, what are you going to tell God about the talents and gifts he gave you? Are you going to be like Adam who tried to blame Eve for his disobedience? You are responsible for your own decisions in your life. I strongly believe that there are men that are going through the same things we women face. There are very good Christian men out there, and I will not let the bad destroy the good name of others.

Not only have our names have been taken away, but society pushes us into the background as well. Always remember that behind every good man is a good woman, and we should not settle for behind, but alongside. Stand by your man and not behind him. I know that any powerful man is due to a woman, whether she is his wife, sister, friend, or mother. For example, in the Bible, Samson was a strong man of God who fell in love with a woman, Delilah, who used and destroyed his life. Delilah shows us that a woman can make or break a man. Another example is King David, whose wife Abigail was a woman of wisdom and compassion. Through her intelligence, David made the right choices and helped determine his destiny. Women are a precious gem from God, given by God to complete our husbands. We need our husbands as much as they need us, if they are good men.

However, a woman should not stay in a relationship where violence is involved because if a man hits a woman once, he will do so again without a doubt. I am not advising women to leave their husbands at the first incident; if the husband is a person who is willing to seek help for his problem then work along with him, while remaining at a safe distance so you can protect yourself as a person and monitor his progress.

Research shows that men who abuse their wives have at some time been abused in their own lives or have witnessed repeated abuse. I can remember George speaking about all the beatings his mother received from their father. I also heard one of his brothers say that the woman whom he was going to marry would receive some of the same beatings his mother received. Men, you are handing down an ancestral spirit to your family. A man who uses his fists and feet on his spouse is a very weak person and feels powerful only when he abuses those around him.

My advice to anyone concerning his wife is to show her lots of love and affection since she is the weaker vessel. That can do wonder, create miracles in the house and around the meal table. Those who believe they don't need to put anything into a marriage and expect to receive everything are living a delusion. Think of a bank account – if nothing is put in, then there is nothing to draw out. Relationships bring high returns on wise investments.

Men, know your heart, and follow it.
Don't wait until your wife departs
"He that finds a wife, finds a good thing"
So why hold back on anything
Live today as the last, and, come tomorrow, live it while it pass
Men, know yourself, and know your heart
Don't wait until your wife departs
Look at her as lilies of the field in the morning dew
That conventional, element of beauty
She looks so pretty and yet so new
Remember her beauty will only last
As long as you shield her from the blast
The midday sun is too strong
You may want to leave her and run
Who will you blame after you return?
To find her back bent in the ground
Men, know your heart, and follow it
Water that flower and nourish it
Love can be as a flower that fades away
And leave memories in your heart to stay
Can you touch memories? Can you embrace it or hear it say
I'll keep you warm when you are cold?
Can it care for you when you are old?
It cannot wipe away the tears

143

When, deep in your heart, you wish that person was there
So, men, know your heart, and follow it
Cherish that flower ❧
And you will always have her.

————◆•◆••◆•◆————

I am thankful that I did not listen to George and stay away from women's groups like he insisted. Over time, I discovered why my preaching husband did not want me to have any friends. When I was alone, it was easy to be weak and confused. I felt I had no choice, but to be a puppet for George. When I joined the women's group, I found I had a voice and independence. I gained not only friends, but also strength.

Following are some letters I received from good friends in Trinidad during my darkest hour of separation from my children. The letters are full of encouragement that lifted my heavy spirit.

Hello Ruth,

I have already caught on. I know you have to make adjustments to your life. God said, "Lo, I am with you always." (Matthew 28:20) He will never forsake or leave you. The Holy Spirit is our greatest comfort. He will advise you, cushion, keep, and protect, and I mean really protect. Love Him; draw closer to Him. Put all of your trust in the Father. If when you cannot see things working out for you, when the road becomes real rough, when everything seems dark, be patient and be still and know your God. When you don't know what to do or what move to make in your situation, ask God for wisdom, and He will give to you freely and abundantly. Remember God answers. Pray; He is mighty, He is the King of Glory. When afflicted, pray; when happy, sing Psalms of praises.

God is a rock when our lives become shaky; He is a shield when everything is coming against you. He is the light, when the bands of wickedness surround you; He is our deliverer in times of stress. The name of the Lord is a strong tower; meet with him in your secret place (His presence). Resist the devil, and he shall flee from you. The devil has no authority over your life because he is a defeated foe. Let God arise in your life, and the enemy be scattered.

I know you need to be strong at this time in your life. I have enclosed a letter from Pastor Frank for you. I will send one from Pastor Brian. I have not received the first letter as yet. I am still awaiting. With God all things are possible.

I shall give you a call, but I have to first clear up some things at TSTT because my bill is very high. When I have cleared up and paid off, I shall call, so please don't think I will not call.

In the meantime I will write to you. Stay faithful to the Father until we talk again. Take courage – God is with you in what you are facing.

Pastor Frances

October 20, 1998

To whom it may concern:

This is to certify that I have known Mr. and Mrs. S. for the past twelve (12) years. I am fully aware of the physical, verbal, and psychological abuse she has experienced from her husband, the said Mr. S.

The extent of the abuse has been transferred to their three children who unknowingly turned against their mother.

My wife, another close friend, and myself have tried to help this family and were viewed by the said Mr. S. as being evil.

She did not make any report to the police because of fear and victimization of her husband. She was fully aware that she was in danger of losing her life, so her only alternative was to leave the marital home to seek a place of refuge and status in your country to protect her life.

Yours respectfully,
Pastor Brent

Be ye therefore perfect, even as your Father which is in heaven is perfect.
Matthew 5:48

Hi Sis,

How are you? So glad to hear from you and rejoice with you that you are alright. You are in my thoughts all the time, so as much as I remember you, I pray for you.

I was just about to write to you when your letter came. That was good timing, because I have seen that your address has changed.

May all God's grace, mercy, and blessings be multiplied to you. God is good; He is with you wherever you go. Even when at times it may seem as though you are not hearing from him. He is too wise to be mistaken and too good to be unkind. God remains Sovereign; He is His Excellency, the only true and living God.

I must tell you that you have made the right decision in leaving, because, since you have been gone, over fifty women have died from their spouses hand; some in the most brutal manner. When I think about the Christian women, I'm glad you got away. Like God did with Joseph and Job, He will restore all that is due to you in time. Trust Him when you don't understand. Some nights ago, I dreamed that I saw your husband, and an older man from St. Vincent was just following him around and making decisions for him. Anyway, we just have to hand him over to the Lord. He needs salvation.

Well, my dear, we are now fully in charge of the young people in the church. Pray for us that God's will be done; my husband is teaching the adults on Sunday morning. I began to understand that our weapons of warfare are not only physical or made with hands; they are spiritual to the pulling down of strongholds in our life. The battleground is in our mind. We have to let God do what we cannot understand and that is to do it all for us.

May God bless and keep you.

Your sis in Christ,
M.K.

March 21, 1997

Hi sis,

How are you? It is good to be writing to you again. I got your last letter with the money in it. I always think of you like Joseph in the Bible. You can go through so much, but you can also benefit from this experience and also learn from it. When everything seem to be not going right for you, the Holy spirit, on the other hand, can be restoring your life, placing it in order, and bringing you on top like Joseph. Do continue to remain faithful and strong.

Joseph did not complain when he was innocently thrown in the pit and also jailed. There was no bitterness or resentment in him. Likewise let the sweetness and love come out from your inner man in spite of your circumstances.

Allow the Holy Spirit to bring comfort, he is the Spirit of comfort, let him give you wisdom, and he is also the Spirit of grace which is sufficient. Be filled with the Holy Spirit and his anointing and he will break the yokes in your past that come to you from time to time. The Father wants to erase them all away from your memory if you leave them with Him. It is the anointing that gives you boldness and helps you to overcome. Don't forget to pray without ceasing on all occasion. Even when you are posting any money down, I want you to bless your wages. Pray for the people you are working with, pray while you are working. Pray for everything, even though it may seem so small. If you are not sure of something, pray. If you feel good, pray. Pray when the memories come flashing back. I'm praying for you most of the time, and I know that God will bring you into top position like Joseph.

Please educate yourself any chance you can. Make the sacrifice to go to night school. Learn all you can. Occupy yourself in your spare time. Make good use of your time because you can be an asset to the Lord.

One day just like that I made up my mind to go to Bible school. I'm ready and very excited. I will be starting in September, and my darling husband decided to go to pray for us.

Enough about me; I saw your children. Their father is doing things he never did for you. He said it is to take the children's mind away from their no good mother. He is doing his best to turn their minds against you. Just pray for them and keep loving them. As a mother, I know how much you love them, but God will give them back to you again. God will make them understand the truth. It's hard to say don't worry, but all you can do is pray. Nothing is impossible with GOD.

Don't hand in, but stand firm and trust God with all you got.

Lots of love from all of us,
Your sis in Christ

--------◆◆◆◆--------

March 16, 1999

Hi my sister,

How are you? I have not heard from you in a long time, is everything alright?

My sister, be of good courage, be patient and God will bring you through. Trust him with all your mind even though you don't understand what is happening around you. I'm praying for you. Even this morning I called your name in my prayer, and I know He will work things out for you. Please forgive me for not writing to you before; I have been very, very busy. I am now counseling our youth on Thursday.

I have been attending conferences; I saw the Word of God that we need to excel in knowledge, love, speech, and giving. I already desired to do this

So what are you doing now? Where are you working? Are you coping? Are you able to earn enough to keep yourself? God is so good; He is more than enough; He is able to bring you out and upwards. Are you still in school? Learn to drive and do all you can for yourself. In time His purpose and plan for your life will come forth.

Everybody is alright. They send their love and warmth to you.

Girl, you have made the right move, because every day a woman dies from domestic violence. It is so bad down here. Women are losing their lives all the time. Our land needs lots of prayer. I know you might have been one of them.

From the pulpit to the parliament, these men who people look up to, down to the bush man, they don't care about the mother of their children.

But thank God for taking you out in time. May God bless and keep you my sister.

Your sister in Christ

———◆◆◆———

January 16, 1997

Hi Sis,

How is everything? I carry the things for the children you send. I give them the same day it arrived. I went up to the house while my husband was talking with their father down the hill. He has them afraid and programmed. He told the children that you are in Trinidad, and I am hiding you at the house. He also tells them to take their mind off you, because you are not a good mother. When he looked around and did not see me, he ran up the hill. He did not want me to talk to the children alone. The three year old tried to look in the bag; his father hit him and told him to move away from it. He said he is not taking anything your many men gave you. He doesn't want another man's money. He shouted, "Tell her I will not be accepting anything that your man buys with his money." I told him you send some money for your older son to buy a bike because he passed this school test, but that did not make him change his mind. We walked away and leave the things. But the money I still have it with me. He sure has a mixed up mind. You sure have a crazy husband, but he looks so sane up on the pulpit.

I will not go with any further details about all he is saying about you. Just trust God to keep you to see your children again. It is time you do something for yourself; you have given this man your all and the best of your youth. Take time for you now. Go back to school, try and laugh a lot I know it will take time for you to learn how to really laugh after all those years around that man. God is good. Stay strong we are praying for you.

Your sis in Christ

149

19

Fire from Ashes

Words that come from the devil are filled with doom and death. Jesus tells us that He has come to give us an abundant life. Some demons come in the name of the Lord to keep children of God down. If you are a man or a woman who is going through the cyclone of evil words from the devil, remember the words of God – "I will never leave you; I have come to give you life."

When I was growing up, I was told that I would never amount to anything. I was told that the man I chose would make me his football. These words flowed into my marriage when George added his version to it and told me that no man would want me for a wife and that he just pitied me.

God is a God of second chances. Remember Abigail in the Bible? (1 Samuel 25:2-42) The story of Esther shows how the devil tried to destroy God's people by sending out words of doom and death. When a child of God holds onto His promises, He always shows that the second chance can be better than the first. I see it as the cleansing rain.

I'm now blessed to be living in the second chance the Lord provided for me. I'm just bathing in His blessings. He has given me everything that I need and more. I have a beautiful home, and as I said before, Jesus makes me laugh. My address is Christian Road in Bloomfield; before Christian Road is Jericho Road. Yes, I can say the walls of my spiritual Jericho have been torn down. Blessed be the name of the Lord!

Before I was born, God had already chosen me. He placed His fire within me; yes, the fire of the Holy Spirit. I see myself as fire from the ash. Many people think that if it looks like ash, that it should be thrown into the wind, forgetting that there is fire before the ash; all that spark needs is something solid to hold onto. Look for the smallest spark in that person next to you. Through God, I'm burning bright. Yes, I'm fire from the ash. The Word of God says, "A bruised reed shall he not break and smoking flax shall not quench, till he sends for judgment unto victory." (Matthew 12:20) I am a woman who has lived to tell the secrets from behind the pulpit.

CPSIA information can be obtained at www.ICGtesting.com
Printed in the USA
LVOW101104161011

250582LV00004B/3/P